Women and
Culture Series

The Women and Culture Series is dedicated to books that illuminate the lives, roles, achievements, and status of women, past or present.

Fran Leeper Buss
Dignity: Lower Income Women Tell of Their Lives and Struggles
La Partera: Story of a Midwife

Valerie Kossew Pichanick
Harriet Martineau: The Woman and Her Work, 1802–76

Sandra Baxter and Marjorie Lansing
Women and Politics: The Visible Majority

Estelle B. Freedman
Their Sisters' Keepers: Women's Prison Reform in America, 1830–1930

Susan C. Bourque and Kay Barbara Warren
Women of the Andes: Patriarchy and Social Change in Two Peruvian Towns

Marion S. Goldman
Gold Diggers and Silver Miners: Prostitution and Social Life on the Comstock Lode

Page duBois
Centaurs and Amazons: Women and the Pre-History of the Great Chain of Being

Mary Kinnear
Daughters of Time: Women in the Western Tradition

Lynda K. Bundtzen
Plath's Incarnations: Woman and the Creative Process

Violet B. Haas and Carolyn C. Perrucci, editors
Women in Scientific and Engineering Professions

Sally Price
Co-wives and Calabashes

Patricia R. Hill
The World Their Household: The American Woman's Foreign Mission Movement and Cultural Transformation, 1870–1920

Diane Wood Middlebrook and Marilyn Yalom, editors
Coming to Light: American Women Poets in the Twentieth Century

Leslie W. Rabine
Reading the Romantic Heroine: Text, History, Ideology

Joanne S. Frye
Living Stories, Telling Lives: Women and the Novel in Contemporary Experience

E. Frances White
Sierra Leone's Settler Women Traders: Women on the Afro-European Frontier

Catherine Parsons Smith and Cynthia S. Richardson
Mary Carr Moore, American Composer

Sierra Leone's Settler Women Traders

Sierra Leone's Settler Women Traders
Women on the Afro-European Frontier

E. Frances White

The University of Michigan Press   Ann Arbor

Copyright © by The University of Michigan 1987
All rights reserved
Published in the United States of America by
The University of Michigan Press and simultaneously
in Markham, Canada, by Fitzhenry and Whiteside
Manufactured in the United States of America

1990   1989   1988   1987   4   3   2   1

Library of Congress Cataloging-in-Publication Data

White, E. Frances.
  Sierra Leone's settler women traders.

  (Women and culture series)
  Bibliography: p.
  Includes index.
  1. Women merchants—Sierra Leone—History—19th century.
2. Women, Black—Employment—Sierra Leone—History—19th
century.   3. Women colonists—Sierra Leone—History—19th
century.   4. Sierra Leone—Economic conditions—To 1896.
I. Title.   II. Series.
HF3933.W47   1987   331.4'81381'09664   86-24997
ISBN 0-472-10080-7 (alk. paper)

To the memory of Sarah Tildon,
Pealine Tildon White, Hollis Tildon,
and James W. White

One morning a woman rose and wrapped her
cloth firmly around her waist and said,
"Today I will bring back something to eat."

And the men began to understand that if
the times were bringing forth a new breed
of men, they were also bringing forth a
new breed of women.

—Ousmane Sembene,
God's Bits of Wood

Preface

Determined to study West African women and recognizing the importance of trade in their lives, I went to Freetown to do a case study of the Big Market. My first visit to the market stunned me, for its pace seemed slow compared to other markets in West Africa. Although the marketplace appeared to have very little business of any consequence, I was encouraged by three research assistants, whose services I obtained through the Institute of African Studies and who helped teach me Krio, to continue working on the Big Market. I soon found that it held an important place among Freetown markets because of the local medicines that its vendors sold. During my eighteen-month stay, I interviewed at least once all of the women holding stalls in the market. Four of these women became major informants whom I often visited while in Sierra Leone.

A picture of the Big Market as a central market in a widespread trading diaspora in the nineteenth century began to emerge. Increasingly my interests shifted to the Krio women's diaspora that spread out from this market. I expanded my interviewing to include anyone willing to talk about Krio women traders. My search took me around the Freetown peninsula to most of the towns that had large Krio populations in the nineteenth century. For most of my interviews outside of the Big Market, I was accompanied by my friend, research assistant, and informant, Mr. I. C. Hotobah-During, an elderly Krio whose knowledge of Krio society proved invaluable.

I returned to Sierra Leone five years later for two months to fill in gaps in my research. Most recently, I spent three months in Sierra Leone and two months in The Gambia to focus on the Krio women's trading network that extended northward into Senegambia. The extent of these women's control over the kola trade to The Gambia shocked me even after eight years of research. I found it hard to believe that no other researchers on the kola trade had noticed the Krio women's part in this, especially since Gambians, with little or no prompting, freely talked about Krio women's involvement in the lucrative kola trade.

On each research trip I supplemented my interviews with work in the valuable Sierra Leone Government Archives. I was surprised to find so much detail about women traders there; fortunately, many nineteenth-century Krio women were literate and wrote to the colonial governor about their trading problems in the hinterland. Thus the Liberated African Letter Books and Local Letters to the Governor contained letters from and about settler women traders. Detailed reports by colonial officials in such documents as the Native Affairs Minute Papers helped fill in many gaps. Finally, travelers' reports and local newspapers added to the picture of Krio women as dynamic traders in the nineteenth century who lost their control of important trade items in the twentieth century. Given the failure of colonial officials to recognize the importance of women's trade, it is not surprising that a summer research trip to London to work in the Public Record Office revealed very little that I had not already learned at the Sierra Leone Government Archives.

This book reflects my growing feminist concerns. On the one hand, it subjects African historiography to a feminist critique by arguing that a full understanding of Sierra Leonean history necessitates an analysis of women's roles. On the other hand, with a lens on African women it examines the feminist theory that grows out of Western experiences yet claims universality. Although I ask questions that reflect larger concerns, I hope that the history of Sierra Leone's settler women traders emerges with all its richness and specialness.

Many have assisted me in the preparation of this book. I received funding from the African American Scholars Council, the Danforth Foundation (Kent Fellowship), and the Roothbert Fund to aid me in my initial research. An A. W. Mellon Faculty Development Grant and a Fulbright Senior Research Scholar Fellowship helped me return to Sierra Leone to collect further material. I am grateful for their support.

I owe a special debt to Adelaide Cromwell, who first suggested I study marketwomen in Sierra Leone and provided advice, guidance, and contacts to begin this study. My graduate professors, Sara Berry, Steve Baier, Margaret Jean Hay, and Filomina Steady, all helped me refine and expand my ideas by providing critical readings of my early writing. It was a pleasure to work with them. My colleagues at Hampshire College, including Miriam Slater and Barbara Yngversson, are responsible for many of the insights that are found in this book. I would also particularly like to thank Margaret Cerullo, Nancy Fitch, Frank Holmquist, Kay Johnson, Nina Payne, and Fredrick Weaver for reading various versions of this manuscript and sharing their criticisms with me. In the process, they helped me to deepen my understanding of feminist historiography and political economy. David Skinner and LaRay Denzer gave me valuable insights from their in-depth knowledge of Sierra Leonean history. Marlyn Silberfein graciously read my manuscript and provided me with helpful suggestions. The encouragement and counsel of Paulla Ebron, who both read this work in many stages and listened to my half-formed ideas, will always be remembered.

Finally, my research in Sierra Leone could never have been completed without the support of many Sierra Leoneans. My research assistants, Mariama Deen, Hassan Bangura, and Sannoh Kamara, helped interpret Sierra Leonean society for me. I will always appreciate their friendship and advice. I am indebted to I. C. Hotabah-During for the entrée he offered into Krio society and to the many Sierra Leoneans who agreed to serve as informants for this study. The Institute of African Studies, Fourah Bay College, where I was a research fellow during my stays in Freetown, provided me with space to work and a congenial atmosphere for intellectual development. Mr. A. W. Short and Dr. C. Magbaily Fyle willingly spent time with me and answered my many questions. Dr. Fyle also read and commented on my work. I appreciate his advice and support.

Contents

Chapter 1

Introduction

The occupation of the [Sierra Leonean] people of all
classes seems . . . to be trading. The female sex, to their
deterioration, lead the way.
          —The Right Reverend E. G. Ingham, 1894

The Right Reverend E. G. Ingham, one-time bishop of Sierra
Leone, expresses the negative attitude that many British administrators and missionaries took toward Sierra Leone's settlers and
their predilection for trading.[1] Like many of his Victorian colleagues, Ingham looked with astonishment and consternation at
the settler women who were actively involved in a sphere that in
Britain was generally reserved for men. Yet although women created a great impression on the European observers of the nineteenth century, they have largely been ignored by the historical
literature on Sierra Leone.[2]

This book is an attempt to refocus attention on this group of
West African women, the women traders of Sierra Leone. A fascinating picture emerges of a group of women, with an unusual
amount of independence, adapting successfully to a new homeland. And although it cannot be argued that these women ever had
the same access to power and wealth that the colony's men had, the
women participated at all levels of society and exerted great influence on the development of Sierra Leone. Central to the definition
of a Sierra Leonean in the nineteenth century was the image of a
stranger-trader; both men and women traded, although they did
not always share the same challenges and opportunities. Men, for
example, were more likely to trade in luxury items than women.
Nonetheless, given the ubiquitous presence of the settler women
traders and their closeness to indigenous cultures through most of
the 1800s, Sierra Leonean history cannot possibly be understood
without examining women.

An unusual opportunity to study the history of African women
stems from the settlers' close relationship to the British. From the

founding of Sierra Leone, the black immigrants to this colony came under the close scrutiny of Europeans who, fortunately, recorded much of what they saw. Thus sufficient archival data exist to reconstruct the history of these women, especially for the nineteenth century. For the early twentieth century, the less abundant but nonetheless useful archival material is combined with oral sources.

Sierra Leone's women should be viewed in the context of the nineteenth- and twentieth-century developments in the Sierra Leone colony and its hinterland. Throughout this period the region was involved in economic and political struggles in which women traders played more than a passive role. Sponsored by a group of British philanthropists that included William Wilberforce, Thomas Clarkson, and Granville Sharpe, the colony had been founded in 1787 by about four hundred black settlers from Great Britain. Members of London's Black Poor, the settlers were both escaping a life of poverty and hoping to contribute to the Christianization of Africa and the establishment of economic alternatives to the slave trade.

The original settlement floundered, but was revived in 1792 by about one thousand black settlers from Nova Scotia. These settlers had supported England during the American Revolution and fled to Nova Scotia with other Whigs. But in Nova Scotia the blacks found their legitimate expectations of receiving farmland dashed. When the newly formed Sierra Leone Company offered them the opportunity to settle in Africa, they accepted the offer as an alternative means of obtaining the opportunities denied them in Nova Scotia.

Their numbers were swelled in 1800 by a group of black Jamaicans, called Maroons, who had fought the British to a standstill and, in compromise treaties, had agreed to settle first in Nova Scotia and subsequently in Sierra Leone. But the bulk of Sierra Leone's population arrived after 1807, when England began openly to suppress the Atlantic slave trade. Slaves intercepted and freed by the British, known as Liberated Africans or Recaptives, were sent to live in villages around the Sierra Leone peninsula. Descendants of these three groups, Nova Scotians, Maroons, and Liberated Africans, make up the ethnic group now known as Krios. Yet as David Skinner and Barbara Harrell-Bond have suggested, in the nineteenth century Krios had not reached enough cohesion to be considered an ethnic group and did not view themselves as such.[3] Rather, they had a dual identity as both Nova Scotians (or Yoruba Recaptives) and Sierra Leoneans. In this book they are called Sierra Leoneans, colony women or men, or settlers when they are referred to as a collective group in the nineteenth century. When trading in the hinterland they became known as Sierra Leoneans; this usage is maintained here. The term *colony* stresses their relationship to the British and will be used for variety. In the past, some authors have used *settler* to refer only to the Nova Scotians and Maroons. Others include all three groups under this rubric. This latter practice is followed here because *settler* conveniently emphasizes the stranger status of all three. It was in the post-1895 era, when the British extended the definition of Sierra Leonean to include peoples of the hinterland, that Krios began perceiving themselves more clearly as a unified ethnic group. The term *Krio* is applied to them only in discussions of that era. Except in direct quotations, the spelling of *Krio* adopted by the historians of Fourah Bay College, University of Sierra Leone, is used rather than the older spelling, Creole. The use of this modern spelling reflects a desire to link the settler community to its African heritage.[4]

Even before Sierra Leone's establishment, its founding fathers postulated economic reasons for its existence, as the colony was conceived partly as an economic alternative to the slave trade. Besides serving as a stage from which to begin Christianizing and "enlightening" Africa, the British philanthropists saw Sierra Leone as an entrée into Africa's vast but untapped market.[5] Soon trade became the main source of Sierra Leone's survival and thus overshadowed all other issues that had influenced the colony's founding. In such a setting the immigrant women's predilection for trading, which came from their West African and Afro-American cultural backgrounds, flourished.[6] And the colony women traded at virtually every level of the economy. Many fulfilled the traditional role of West African women as produce traders, taking the produce of their husbands or other African farmers to market in Freetown and the surrounding villages. They also competed as economic intermediaries in the trade between Europe and Sierra Leone's hinterland.[7] Like colony men, these women rarely felt constrained to remain agricultural peasants, as some of the founding fathers would have preferred. Instead they used their freedom to travel and trade up-country. This independence gave the settlers as a group advantages over other Africans who had to overcome strong ties to their land and families in order to have the mobility necessary for trading over long distances. Further, settler women had advantages over other African women, for they were not as constrained by traditional family roles that required women to stay close to home.

For many of the settler women, economic independence was accompanied by a degree of control over their own sexuality unusual for the nineteenth century. The history of the various groups that came to comprise the Krios illustrates the complex relationship between economic and sexual independence. As shall be made clear in chapter 2, Nova Scotian women arrived with expectations of economic autonomy and relative sexual independence as measured by their ability to move in and out of marriage bonds with relative ease, while Maroon women settlers were accustomed to relatively inflexible marriage bonds and little economic independence.

Differences based on class also characterized the settler women's varying experiences. Elite women were more confined by Victorian models of the good Christian wife than were most other women.[8] Nonetheless, the prevailing tendency in nineteenth-century settler society was for settler women to have more economic freedom than indigenous women. As one Mandingo woman made clear to Winwood Reade, a British adventurer exploring West Africa, women could be free of their husbands in Freetown; she insisted that there they could escape "woman palaver."[9] Freetown, then, became a symbol of liberation for indigenous women who wanted to escape from patriarchal, patrilocal kinship systems that bound them over to the control of their husbands and senior wives.

As settler women traveled up-country to trade, their newly established identity as Sierra Leoneans enabled them to set up trading networks.[10] Moreover, they were able to exploit their relationship with the British to tie the networks to European commercial firms both in Sierra Leone and abroad. The Sierra Leoneans saw these commercial possibilities long before the British would admit to them. That settler women participated in this trade despite the pervasive sexist attitudes of European colonial officials and traders further underscores the aggressive way in which Sierra Leonean women sought out the role of economic intermediary.[11] This is not to suggest that the sexist attitude of the British was not a liability for settler women, however. In spite of their enterprising attitudes, Sierra Leonean women found their economic opportunities severely limited by the sexism of both European and African traders. Notwithstanding these liabilities, which cannot be overstated, the women did have certain advantages over their men. While in the hinterland, for example, the women often found it easier to integrate into the host culture. Sometimes they gained the protection of their hosts through marriage; and some became so well integrated that a traveler would find it difficult to distinguish them from other wives. An important part of their participation in the host culture was the willingness of some settler women to join the women's secret societies, known as *Bundu* or *Sande*. Colony women used the societies as an entrée into their host's culture, but for the most part settler men refused to join the men's secret society, *Poro*.[12] Participation in Bundu became an important tool in establishing trading relationships.

Facing the same liabilities as their men and in a time of increasing competition from European traders, Sierra Leonean women were unable to sustain their economic successes into the twentieth century. Through the nineteenth century, the settlers and British had developed good trading relations, and the Sierra Leoneans prospered. Some men and women even began trading directly with Europe, importing textiles and trinkets and exporting palm produce and kola nuts. Toward the turn of the century, however, Britain changed its attitude toward Africa and began to undermine the settlers' economic position. The Sierra Leoneans had considered themselves as equal partners with the British, but the beginning of the colonial era was accompanied by a new wave of racism that did not permit the British to recognize any Africans as equals. In 1898 the protectorate peoples struck out at the newly imposed colonialism. In southern Sierra Leone, too weak to confront the British directly, they attacked the visible representatives of the British, the settler traders and missionaries. Following this crisis, the British crystallized their policy of undermining the settlers' position by bypassing them in trade and dislodging them from upper-level civil service positions. Consequently the Krios lost their economic intermediary role to Lebanese traders who had begun arriving in Sierra Leone in the late nineteenth century. Not only did settler women lose out in the hinterland trade, they also lost their predominant role in Freetown's produce trade. At the wholesale level, they were challenged by both Lebanese merchants and European firms. At the retail level, they were challenged by African women of other ethnic backgrounds, especially Temne.

A decline in sexual autonomy accompanied the settler women's economic decline. Women's loss of control over their sexuality was reflected in marriage bonds less flexible than those of many settler women in the nineteenth century. One response to declining fortunes was to form a close-knit ethnic group, a choice that required greater control over women's sexuality. Many women resisted these efforts at control; nonetheless, an ideological battle was waged that attempted to restrict women's independence. The Victorian wife increasingly became the model against which all women were measured.

A Historiographic View

In recent years African historiography has been moving away from presenting the contact between European and African culture from the dominant white (and ultimately racist) perspective that has characterized academic discourse since the nineteenth century. In certain important areas, however, this change has yet to occur, as some historians still fail to recognize the strength of African culture in the face of the conquering Europeans. This book stands as a critique of this failure of Sierra Leonean historiography and attempts to correct the problem by expanding the traditional view of Sierra Leonean settler history to include settler women. It moves the emphasis from elite males, both European and African, and presents the settlers as Africans accommodating themselves to an African milieu. By including a wider spectrum of African settler society than earlier historians, this work also demonstrates that in Sierra Leone culture borrowing flowed not only between the indigenous African and European frontier people but also between these two groups and the nonindigenous, heterogeneous African settler population.

It is the complexity of social change in Sierra Leone that most historians of the Krios have failed to address.[13] In part, the failure to recognize these complexities stems from the tendency of Africanist historians to ignore the boundaries between ethnic groups altogether. Fredrik Barth has addressed himself to the need to "shift the focus of investigation from internal constitution and history of separate groups to ethnic boundaries and boundary maintenance."[14] Within this shifted focus, ethnicity still remains important but appears less rigidly maintained than a more narrow perspective would allow. Therefore, such an approach places the settlers in the larger, African context of Sierra Leonean society and economy and highlights those people who cross the ethnic boundaries between settler and indigenous African populations.

Further historiographical problems are implicit in the failure to recognize complexities of social change and cultural contact. For example, such a failure demonstrates the elitist tendencies of historians who recognize only the actions of elite African and European males. The study of history from the top down has been criticized in European and American history.[15] Historians of these regions have responded to the criticism and gone far in studying lower class people, especially in urban and demographic history. The recent emphasis on slavery in Africa also reflects this trend. Yet many who study Africa remain attached to a view of African history that pays attention only to its most elite participants, a shortcoming reflected in Sierra Leonean historiography's emphasis on those settlers who most successfully assimilated Western values. For example, while J. D. Hargraves's biography of the great barrister Sir Samuel Lewis is a valuable contribution to Sierra Leonean historiography, such a study presents only one of many possible views of the past.[16] The limitations of this approach become especially apparent when a broader perspective is adopted; for Hargraves, having failed to recognize the cultural contact points and place Lewis in a wider context, makes the gulf between the settlers and indigenous populations appear much greater than it actually was.[17]

To understand the African impact on settler culture one must return to the foundation of Kriodom, for it is at the very beginning of this history that historians first fail to recognize the strength of African culture and its impact on the future Krios. A reassessment of the culture the Black Loyalists of Nova Scotia took with them to Sierra Leone demonstrates that their lives had been profoundly influenced by Africa even before they left the New World.

Two recent works address the Nova Scotian roots of Krio culture.[18] Both authors, James Walker and Ellen G. Wilson, provide clear insights into the important influences of settler culture on the evolution of Krio society. Some of the Western influences that have been attributed to British culture actually came from the Afro-American culture of the Nova Scotian and Maroon settlers. Although they were few in number, the settlers set the early standards of Sierra Leonean/indigenous contact. As Walker argues, rather than aping European ways, Nova Scotians were acting in accordance with their American and Sierra Leonean experiences.[19]

Yet although Walker and Wilson rightly reject the notion that Nova Scotians imitated British culture, both ignore the impact of West African traditions on Nova Scotian culture in Sierra Leone. Their oversight appears especially glaring when it is realized that the Nova Scotian community comprised not merely African descendants but also native-born Africans. As both authors note, some of the Nova Scotians were returning to villages that they remembered; but neither Walker nor Wilson recognize that African culture must have influenced the development of Afro–Nova Scotian culture, not only in America but in Sierra Leone as well.

Wilson argues that once the Nova Scotians had arrived in Africa, they did not identify with the Africans living there. Instead, they viewed Britain as their homeland and thought of themselves as British North Americans with African ancestry.[20] No doubt when the Nova Scotians returned to Africa, they had been so profoundly affected by their North American experience that African culture appeared alien. And in their need to establish an identity, they emphasized their Americanness.[21] But the culture that they evolved was a synthesis of African, British, and American cultures.

Peter H. Wood has written persuasively on African survivals in Afro-American culture. In particular, his discussion of eighteenth-century South Carolina sheds light on the Nova Scotians' culture because, as Walker points out, most of the settlers came from South Carolina and Virginia.[22] Wood notes that most historians missed the significance of the facts that colonial South Carolina's population was largely black and its immigrants were largely West African. These immigrants brought with them, for example, their pharmacopoeia, easily transferred because of climatic similarities. Most significantly for those Nova Scotians who later ended up on Africa's Windward Coast, the immigrants brought knowledge of rice farming. Wood notes that several references exist that demonstrate the slaves' familiarity with rice:

> Those Africans who were accustomed to growing rice on one side of the Atlantic, and who found themselves raising the same crop on the other side, did not markedly alter their annual routine.[23]

Indeed, South Carolina women used a mortar and pestle technique in processing rice that was "strikingly close [in] resemblance" to the West African method.[24] These are influences that previously have been overlooked because of a tendency to accept without question the belief that Western culture and technology completely overwhelmed African culture and technology and that influences flowed only in one direction. It is fair to assume, however, that when Nova Scotians returned to West Africa, they took with them a culture already influenced by African culture.

That this African-American cultural synthesis took place in America naturally affected the form in which it emerged. Moreover, these were experiences that all shared. The harsh realities of North American life meant that many women and men had to learn how to survive without the full support of their natural families. By the time the Black Loyalists escaped to Nova Scotia, the North American experience had reinforced and strengthened the West African traditions of independence for women. Thus, as Walker points out, in the Nova Scotian communities family life was characterized by flexible marital bonds and lack of "concern for formal conjugality."[25] Although marital bonds often lacked legal sanction, long-term relationships were recognized. These relationships, however, were flexible enough to allow Nova Scotian women the necessary mobility to participate in trade.

While the Nova Scotians brought to Sierra Leone an altered African culture, the Recaptives came firmly grounded in West African traditions. Consequently their connection to the indigenous cultures was more visible. Indeed, the very diversity of the Liberated African community allowed for several connections between colony culture and the indigenous cultures.

In their 1977 article, David Skinner and Barbara Harrell-Bond call for studies that would focus on the stratified and ethnically diverse nature of Krio society.[26] As Skinner and Harrell-Bond have pointed out, historians have tended ". . . to project the existence of a homogeneous Christian, westernized society from the 1950s back to the 1850s."[27] This tendency to read the present into the past makes the gulf between settlers and other ethnic groups seem greater than it actually was in the nineteenth century. In reality, Sierra Leoneans were a people of diverse origins who defined their ethnic backgrounds as Yoruba, Igbo, Mandingo, etc., rather than as Krios. While some Sierra Leoneans were distinguished by their religion, dress, and place of permanent residence, these distinctions could also characterize indigenous peoples. Some gained access to Sierra Leonean status through a ward system in which the colony-born took hinterland children into their homes. By staying in settler homes, wards gained access to Western education, Christian instruction, and Western-influenced life-styles, advantages that aided in the Afro-European contact and commerce.[28]

But alternative routes to settler identity also existed. By simply living in the colony, one could learn settler dress styles and customs. Since English was spoken around Sierra Leone before the colony's establishment, indigenous peoples easily learned Krio (an African-based language with a mixture of languages including English, Yoruba, and Temne—also spelled *Creole*). To complete the identity, one took an English name and began trading. In the nineteenth century, to be Sierra Leonean meant to be a trader and/or a member of a universalistic religion (Christianity or Islam) who looked to Freetown as a source of political authority.

While the seeds had been sown for the distinctive ethnic group that emerged in the twentieth century, during the first hundred years of the colony's existence the settlers' diversity enabled them to function as a bridge between African and European culture. From the British, settlers learned about Christianity, the English language, Western dress styles, and new occupations.[29] Influences from the indigenous cultures included loan words, technological

adaptations to the environment, food preferences, local pharmacology, and philosophy. Such influences reached colony culture
through people who changed their identity to Sierra Leonean or
broadened their identity to include being Sierra Leonean without
completely relinquishing their Mende, Temne, or other ethnic
identity. The adoption of Sierra Leonean identity by indigenous
peoples therefore influenced settler development as indigenous
people brought with them their own cultural backgrounds.

Others have criticized the traditional historiography for over-
looking this diversity in settler culture. In 1968, John Peterson
published an article that went far in correcting misconceptions
about the Sierra Leone settlers.[30] In particular, Peterson criticizes
earlier accounts that, while concentrating on the Sierra Leonean
elite, characterized the entire culture as imitation English.[31] Yet
despite Peterson's critical article and the publication in the following year of his dissertation focusing on the African influences in
settler culture,[32] historians continue to underemphasize the complexities of Sierra Leonean culture. In a 1971 article, Abner Cohen
suggests that it is no exaggeration to call Krios black Englishmen.[33]
Two years later, Leo Spitzer describes as an imitation of Victorian
England the social life of the colony upper class, whose attitudes he
felt reflected the "broader spectrum of Creole society."[34] Even
though Spitzer and Cohen claim to recognize the syncretic development of Krio culture, they focus mainly on British influences.
Missing from their accounts is an appreciation of the richness of
Krio culture that stems from its multifarious roots. Besides the
impact of the original Sierra Leone settlers, settler culture reflected
the influence of the various ethnic origins of the Krio people. Most
important among these influences was Yoruba culture, as the
Yoruba predominated among the Liberated Africans. But Igbo
culture also influenced settlers, and recaptured slaves brought with
them cultural traditions from all over West Africa and as far away
as Angola.

When the analysis of Sierra Leonean history is extended to include Liberated African women, the influence of African culture
becomes more obvious. Although rarely reaching the economic
heights of the most prosperous Sierra Leonean men, women
played an important role in the economic drama of the nineteenth

century. Many of these women came originally from Yorubaland, where women traditionally traveled far and wide while pursuing their trade.[35] Once in Sierra Leone, they continued to market their husbands' produce as they had done in their homeland. Thus Liberated African women felt as free as their Nova Scotian sisters to travel to the interior to trade.

When in the interior, women oscillated between identifying as a special ethnic group from the colony and adapting to local cultures. These were not always conscious decisions because Sierra Leonean women were deeply affected by local culture. In part, their identification with local culture came about because many of the Recaptives had been born in the region. Although peoples from the coastal region of present-day Nigeria and Benin predominated among the Recaptives, those from Temne, Mende, and Loko proved influential in Sierra Leone because they came from the surrounding local cultures. Furthermore, the Recaptives mixed with the local populations on which they relied heavily for food.

Settler women learned about indigenous culture when they joined the female secret societies such as Bundu. In these societies they were instructed in the philosophical and moral beliefs of the indigenous culture and were able to share experiences with indigenous women and to learn from them. When colony women traveled into the interior, many adopted the ways of their host culture, such as indigenous dancing, hairstyles, and cooking techniques. In addition, they participated in the religious life of the community. Settler women were eclectic in their new land. They learned about Christianity and used it to aid in their advancement as a group. But they found the philosophies learned in Bundu helpful, too. Bundu connections, which are discussed further in chapter 2, are relevant here because they demonstrate the influence of indigenous culture on settler development and suggest that Krio cultural roots were more complex and diverse than traditionally granted.

Given the nebulousness of the Sierra Leonean identity in the nineteenth century, interior women found it easy to claim colony connections when it aided their trading ventures. Sierra Leonean women had important connections in port towns and understood the commercial environment. Not surprisingly, indigenous women wanted to identify with such groups. But interior women did not completely give up their cultural background. On the contrary, by contributing to the spread of Bundu and other institutions they aided in the diffusion of indigenous culture into Liberated African society.

The Status of Women

This book's focus on women does more than highlight settler connections in indigenous cultures, thus contributing to the revision of Sierra Leonean history; it also adds to the feminist discourse on gender and the cross-cultural understanding of the status of women. The combination of strong archival material from the nineteenth century and oral histories about the early twentieth century provides rich sources from which to study changing status over time. The results from this study challenge the Western-biased categories that have found their way into much of the emerging feminist canon comparing women's status across cultures.

Many feminists influenced by the Marxist tradition of studying political economy have attempted to subsume the study of women under the study of class. For these scholars, women's relationship to a society's productive forces determine their status. For example, Karen Sacks, in *Sisters and Wives: The Past and the Future of Sexual Equality,* focuses on the impact of changing modes of production on women's position in Africa.[36] Making clear her debt to Frederick Engels,[37] she argues that as the mode of production increases in complexity, women's status deteriorates. In supporting their evolutionary schemas, both Sacks and Engels overlook the ways culture shapes changes in the social relations of production. The experience of Sierra Leonean women suggests that changes in the mode of production do affect relations between women and men, but in more complex ways than these authors assume; for cultural and religious beliefs and women's various economic and social positions in the already existing society intrude into the new formulations of sexual relations that emerge from changes in the mode of production.[38]

Krio women's history illustrates this point well. Nineteenth-century Sierra Leone witnessed increasing economic sophistication as trade between the colony and its hinterland evolved. Yet for many Liberated African women, their involvement in the era of merchant capitalism led to increased economic and sexual independence. The slave trade that displaced these women to Freetown disrupted the cultural and religious constraints on them sufficiently to allow them to expand the West African tradition of female independence far beyond what had been acceptable before.

Many women, however, were unable to sustain this freedom into the twentieth century. Religious and cultural traditions based on myths about Krio heritage were used to erode women's independence. Facing the loss of opportunities to participate in a new economy characterized by finance capitalism, most Krio women retreated to lives of poverty, becoming petty traders, taking Western-style female jobs, and/or depending on men. The decline in status for Krio women, however, opened up avenues for Temne women to replace them in trade and thus strengthen their economic position within Sierra Leone. The impact of the changing economy on women was far from uniform. The failure to recognize the complex ways a changing political economy affects women's status grows out of both a bias in Marxist traditions that sees women only in relationship to their economic status and a misguided approach that attempts to isolate one factor that affects women's status universally.

Others have similarly oversimplified when they have posed an opposition between public and private spheres as a basis for the existence of a near-universal sexual asymmetry. For example, Sherry Ortner and Harriet Whitehead, basing themselves on earlier work by Michelle Rosaldo,[39] have recently offered a persuasive statement on the cultural construction of sexuality and gender that recognizes the ways kinship and marriage help to construct sexual identity and sexuality, most notably heterosexuality.[40] But like Rosaldo, they also argue that the key to the universal male domination of women lies in men's control over the public realm and women's relegation to the private. This formulation, however, ignores the way public and private remained intertwined in West Africa, as power in the public sphere grew out of kinship relationships in the private sphere.[41] Moreover, many West African women have participated in public life and have wielded power and authority in such key areas as the marketplace. Collectively, through female solidarity groups such as Sierra Leone's Bundu societies, women have played crucial roles in government.[42] Ortner and Whitehead have imposed Western terms on non-Western women as they place public and private domains in an opposition that does not make sense when applied to many African societies.

In an important correction to her own thesis, Rosaldo later recognizes further shortcomings in positing a public/private opposition as an explanation for the unversality of gender hierarchy. In this later work she argues that the content and implications of sexual inequalities varies too greatly to be explained by a universal cause.[43] Thus efforts by feminist scholars to make cross-cultural comparisons of women's status have been doomed to failure by the questions they have asked. In search of a universal basis on which to judge women's status, these scholars look for isolated causes (such as the development of private property or a private/public split) while failing to recognize that women's status is derived from a constellation of social, political, and economic factors that interact to give meaning to women's activities. As this work on Sierra Leonean women demonstrates, the various components of ascribed status, such as women's treatment by their husbands, their role in kinship and marriage, and their relative participation in production, are all factors that should be taken into account when studying women's position. Furthermore, while many of these factors may be, and probably are, interrelated, it should not be assumed that all rise and fall together or form part of a "seamless web." When this is understood, it becomes clear that economic autonomy might mean one thing in nineteenth-century Sierra Leone and another in twentieth-century Britain because many other factors (e.g., state power, sexual independence, religion, class structure) interact with this autonomy to give it specific meaning.

This study also demonstrates that relationships among and between women and men should form a central part of any analysis on female status. Equally important is the connection between the family and other issues such as class, ethnicity, and religion. With this perspective, women no longer appear to be passive creatures shaped by the family, an institution that in reality they actively help to create. Instead, as Rosaldo suggests, the family becomes a part of the wider social context in which women and men interact.[44]

This historical examination of Sierra Leone's settler women traders unearths the configuration of social forces that determine women's status, highlighting both the relationships and contradictions between these forces. It looks at Sierra Leonean society at various stages of integration into the world capitalist economy but does not ignore kinship relations, marriage patterns and, to the extent possible, women's sexuality. Chapter 2 begins the historical narrative and follows it until 1898, a watershed in Sierra Leonean economic and political history. Chapter 3 continues the narrative through World War II. Using the biographical tool so valuable to social historians, chapter 4 focuses on three women traders, highlighting the ways women were prepared for their trading careers, the close connections between settler women and indigenous Africans, and the business exploits of a highly successful trader. Finally, chapter 5 returns to questions about the changing and varying status of women, provides a comparative perspective, and summarizes and discusses the study's conclusions.

Chapter 2

Confronting Freedom:
A New Breed of Woman

In March, 1794, fifteen shiploads of Nova Scotian blacks arrived at St. George's Bay, Sierra Leone. They emigrated with the hope of reviving a floundering colony of black settlers from England and securing the farmland and political freedoms that had been unjustly denied them in Nova Scotia. Having accepted the offer of the Sierra Leone Company to settle in West Africa, they expected to be full partners in a mission to civilize, Christianize and cultivate Africa. The company's concern that the colony should be profitable, however, overshadowed their humanitarian concerns for the black loyalists. Although humanitarian interests were important for the company, Sierra Leone was foremost a commercial venture.[1] Despite false starts, the British government took control of the colony in 1807, and it became a wedge in Britain's expanding economic empire.

The colony's foundation occurred at a crucial turning point in Britain's economic history.

> As Britain changed from a mercantile to an industrial capitalist nation, so also West Africa changed from being a simple supplier of slaves for the merchant traders to being a market for the industrialists.[2]

No longer was the West African coast seen as a source of labor for plantation colonies in the New World. Britain's need for raw materials to fuel her developing industries was growing. Palm oil, palm kernels, and peanuts outstripped slaves in value. The late eighteenth and early nineteenth centuries witnessed a new era of economic expansion. Slowly but steadily, Britain moved to expand markets where her cheap manufactured goods could be exchanged for the raw materials necessary for the manufacturing of those goods. Taking advantage of technological developments such as the steamship, the submarine cable, quinine prophylaxis, and breechloaders, the world's largest thalassocracy was beginning to emerge.[3]

From the beginning the black settlers, placed on center stage of part of the Afro-European frontier, played an integral role in Britain's expansionist policies. Often the British doubted the need for the settler's role, and unquestionably the settlers never lived up to British expectations; but for the first century of the colony's existence, these early settlers and the Liberated Africans who followed them proved an invaluable factor in economic expansion. When the British were unable to staff their administrative posts throughout West Africa, the Sierra Leoneans filled in. Venturing into the hinterland, they established some of the first commercial links between the African peasantry and the European merchants.

In forging links with the people in the hinterland, the settlers found people who were willing not only to trade with the colony but also often to initiate trading relations.[4] The picture that emerges in the early stages of colony-hinterland relations is one of both sides attempting to expand trade. Interior peoples balanced their concern about British anti-slavery activity against their desire for manufactured goods while the colony struggled to establish itself as more important than the other central marketplaces throughout the Sierra Leone–Guinea region.

Long before the colony's foundation a lively Afro-European and intra-African trade had been firmly established. Large movements of people responding to this trade had peopled the region with several Mande-speaking peoples as well as Class and Kru speakers.[5] For example, during the seventeenth century Mandinka related to the Soso began moving into what became the Solima Yalunka Kingdom in the eighteenth century.[6] Based at Fabala, these Mande speakers were to establish caravan routes to Freetown.[7]

The Solima Yalunka Kingdom was one part of the Sierra Leone–Guinea system so important to the colony's development. Allen Howard has described this system in the most detail.[8] According to Howard, the Sierra Leone–Guinea system grew out of the slave trade era and is composed of four ecological zones: "the Sierra Leone–Guinea plain, the uplands and hill country bordering the plain, the Futa Jallon, and the upper Niger river basin."[9] While trade routes emerged to facilitate movement of slaves to the coast, the four ecologically complementary zones also developed a flourishing intraregional trade. For example, salt, fish, and swamp rice were sent from the coast to the Futa region, which in turn sent cattle and other livestock to the coast.[10] Into this commercial system intruded the Sierra Leone Colony as Freetown successfully pulled the bulk of overseas trade through its port and reoriented this trade from slaves to raw materials.[11]

The Nova Scotians, Maroons, and Liberated Africans

Nova Scotian women arrived in Sierra Leone with a historical and cultural background that allowed them to participate in the Sierra Leone–Guinea system's trade to a degree that amazed their British contemporaries. Both their African roots and their American experiences had affected Nova Scotian women. From African culture came a sense of economic autonomy that was rarely found in contemporary European women. Sidney Mintz and Richard Price have argued that West African women had a deep-rooted cultural predilection to be economically autonomous from their men. They point out that when looking at the evolution of Afro-American sex roles, it is not important exactly what form this economic autonomy took (i.e., marketing or farming); rather, it is important that people held a general belief about the form of sex roles. Afro-Jamaican women took up trading in the post-slavery era not because their female ancestors traded in Africa, but because they had maintained a culturally based notion of how women should behave economically within the family. Of course, not only was the notion of economic autonomy compatible with the Jamaican slave system, but it was also reinforced by that system.[12]

In other words, Afro–Nova Scotians and their forbears had arrived in North America with certain notions about female behavior within the family. They did not expect that their men should be largely responsible for providing food or redistributing that food around the community. Slavery's harsh lessons reinforced these notions. And as the Black Loyalists followed their British liberators to Nova Scotia, they found that harsh conditions there also necessitated female autonomy.

Related to this attitude of self-reliance was the existence of flexible marriage bonds among the Nova Scotians. The old notion that Afro-American slaves had no marriage institution has been laid to rest by Gutman, Genovese, and many others.[13] Indeed, the average family that emigrated to Sierra Leone consisted of a married couple with three children.[14] Nonetheless it appears that divorce was frequent, and by 1802 one-third of the Nova Scotian households were female headed.[15] In part, the high incidence of divorce paralleled practices found in much of coastal West Africa. The Sierra Leone region, however, did not share in this liberal practice. Usually, indigenous women could obtain divorces only if they could prove their husbands' cruelty or impotence. Moreover, most groups followed levirate marriage practices, and there was little women could do to resist unless they could refund their bridewealth.[16] In contrast, Nova Scotian women had the freedom to break marriage bonds without the obligations stemming from bridewealth payments and family pressure.

Black Loyalist culture was also marked by an evolving Afro-American Christianity, an evolution that gave support to the Afro-American adaptation to monogamy. Yet clearly this Afro-American religion combined Christianity with African beliefs and rituals. Blassingame has indicated that black Christianity served as the form for many African retentions.[17] Black Nova Scotian culture formed just as this religious synthesis was beginning. Among the Nova Scotians' most influential men was David George, a co-founder of one of America's earliest black churches.[18]

More important than churches such as those built by George were nighttime religious meetings held by slaves. Rawick has given us vivid accounts of these meetings in the nineteenth century and has shown how the form of these meetings was closely associated with African religious practices.[19] These prayer meetings, however, had eighteenth-century roots. An important early settler, Mary Perth, secretly attended and helped lead nocturnal slave meetings called for study and religion while she was a slave in Virginia; she carried her religious convictions with her to Nova Scotia.[20] Confronting the problems of racism, economic depressions, and harsh winters, the Nova Scotians chose their religious leaders as their community leaders. Men and women such as Mary

Perth and David George represented the concerns of their people to the authorities and watched over their community's spiritual needs in Nova Scotia and Sierra Leone.

The imprint of New World experience can be seen in the flexible marriage bonds, monogamy, and attachment to Christianity exhibited by the Nova Scotians, all factors that prepared them to participate in Afro-European trade. From the beginning the Nova Scotians complained about restrictions that the Sierra Leone Company placed on trading. The settlers viewed trading as the logical way to survive in the absence of viable farms. While John Clarkson, the first Sierra Leone governor, looked askance at their commercial inclinations, the realities of their situation prevailed and the company yielded to settler pressure.[21] Almost immediately a flourishing trade developed between the fledgling colony and the surrounding peasants. Restrictions remained, however, on retail trading, which the company reserved as a monopoly. Finally, in 1794, the company yielded to settler pressure and the need for a more efficient retailing system and agreed to license settlers for the retail trade. Three of the first six licensees were women: Mary Perth, Sophia Smalls, and Martha Hazeley.[22]

Of these three, Mary Perth's life story is best known. By the time she received her license to trade, she had reached her early fifties, having begun life as a slave in Virginia.[23] During the revolutionary war she escaped to British lines and arrived in Nova Scotia with three children from her master's plantation in Norfolk. In Sierra Leone, Perth was prosperous enough to take her ailing daughter to England; in preparation for the journey, she sent £150 to Henry Thornton, chairperson of the Sierra Leone Company, to invest for use during their stay.[24] Perth's outstanding character brought her to the attention of the British public through descriptions of her piety in the missionary journal *Evangeline Magazine*.[25]

Zachary Macaulay, governor of Sierra Leone from 1796 to 1799, relied on her skill with children and had her manage his household and look after his African children. In 1799 he took her to England to care for the children. In her early sixties, Perth returned to Sierra Leone in 1801. But her working days were not yet over, as she provided meals for Church Missionary Society clergy. She still must have been a lively woman when she married her second husband on February 13, 1806.[26]

Less is known about the details of Sophia Smalls's life, but evidence suggests that she, too, prospered. By 1796 she was able to build Sierra Leone's first two-story house, which cost her £150. She let the house to missionaries. In addition to her retail license, Smalls obtained one of only two licenses to sell liquor available in the colony.[27] Both Perth and Smalls were victims of looting during the French occupation of Freetown from September 28 to October 13, 1794. This was a major setback for them in their first year in business, as their goods had been bought on credit.[28] That they were able to survive this misfortune was a sign of their commercial ability.

The early days were prosperous ones for Nova Scotian women, but prosperity was short-lived. By 1820, few were in business. In 1818 the only Nova Scotian woman trading up-country on a large scale was Charlotte Simpson. She was so successful that she had built a ten-ton boat that she used for trading.[29] By the 1840s the Nova Scotians' economic eclipse was complete; in her book published in 1849, Elizabeth Melville describes the Nova Scotian women not as traders but as sick nurses.[30] They also were laundresses and seamstresses as well as important property owners.

The trading eclipse of the Nova Scotian women was one aspect of the general decline of Nova Scotian fortunes in Sierra Leone. Much of the trade in which both the women and the men had engaged seemed large by the standards of the colony's early days; but as trade with the hinterland increased in volume, they found it difficult to compete successfully. Unable to break a European monopoly on the import and export trade, the Nova Scotians had to obtain their trade goods from European merchants. Moreover, because of limited capital the Nova Scotian traders were forced to secure their trading items on credit, putting them at a disadvantage compared to their European competitors.[31] As the economy expanded, the Nova Scotians attempted to expand the scale of their operations. Anxious to compete with the European merchants who were squeezing small traders out of business, the Nova Scotians overextended themselves and defaulted on their credit arrangements with the European firms.[32] They were forced out of trade.

While the men turned to government employment as a substitute for commerce, the women provided domestic services to the European community; both men and women relied on property acquired through their trading successes and from their original company allotments for extra income. With a growing European merchant and civil service population, Nova Scotians profited by renting out houses.

The Nova Scotians were replaced economically by the Jamaican Maroons who arrived in Sierra Leone in 1800. The remarkable history of these Maroons has captured the attention of several historians.[33] These escaped slaves fought the British to a standstill. Jamaica, with its mountainous landscape, was well-suited for these guerrilla soldiers; they harassed Jamaican plantation society almost to the point of hysteria during the 1720s and 1730s. The ability of escaped slaves to remain free in a society where freedom for blacks was to be granted only by whites threatened to undermine slave-based Jamaican society.

Unlike the Nova Scotians, who lived in a predominantly white society, the Maroons had little contact with whites; for Jamaican Maroon society had a much larger proportion of African-born members.[34] The Maroons returned to Africa, then, with a culture that was quite distinct from that of the Nova Scotians'. Differences in sex roles, marriage structure, and religion reflected these distinctions.

Sidney Mintz and Richard Price have argued that Afro-Jamaicans maintained a cultural belief in female economic autonomy.[35] Yet the Maroon society's evolution led to a different development even though continual contact occurred between the slaves and the escapees. Runaway slave societies evolved in reaction to the conditions of living in opposition to the dominant power structure. Thus although Maroon women farmed much as women in West Africa did, the former lived separately with their children in special protected villages while the men remained poised to fight.[36]

The special circumstances of the Maroons also forced them to face the problem of serious sexual imbalance. As in most slave societies, more men ran away than women. While the Maroons often raided plantations to obtain more women, the sexual imbalance remained; the problem was exacerbated by the prevailing polygynous marriage structure. The Maroons were forced to create rules to lessen competition for women. Among the Leeward Maroons who eventually migrated to Sierra Leone, men shared sexual rights in women while the primary rights to a woman's labor and her children were retained by one man. This arrangement left room for women to have a great deal of freedom to form sexual relationships outside of their marriages.[37] Thus the structure of the Maroon marriage institution also differed greatly from that of the Nova Scotians.

Finally, the Maroons differed from Nova Scotians in their religious orientation. Christianity had made little impact on Afro-Jamaicans during this early period, and African religious beliefs—or the amalgamation of several African religious traditions—had a stronger impact on Jamaican culture than on Nova Scotian society. Consequently there developed no religious tradition that might support the development of Western marriage practices.

Tensions between one group of Maroons (the Trelawney Town Maroons) and the government broke out in 1795 and resulted in the group's removal to Nova Scotia.[38] Dissatisfied with Nova Scotia, the Maroons agreed to settle in Sierra Leone.[39] For the British, the Trelawney Town Maroons arrived at an opportune time, as these seasoned soldiers used their military prowess to assist in quelling a Nova Scotian rebellion.

Certain aspects of Maroon life, however, disturbed the British. Of most concern to them were Maroon marriage practices. Even before the Maroons' arrival in Sierra Leone, the British attempted to dissuade them from practicing polygyny. Commenting on an attempt in Nova Scotia by the British to convince the Maroons that European-style marriage was preferable, R. C. Dallas reports that

> none of the wives could be persuaded to resign her right to her husband, and the girls were so riotous and noisy in their objection to taking any *swear* [oath], declaring without qualification they would not.[40]

Once the Maroons were in Sierra Leone the British attempted to regulate their marriages through legal means. Married men were prohibited from increasing the number of their wives while unmarried men were restricted to one wife.[41] At least for the first part of the nineteenth century, the Maroons simply ignored the British laws.

Despite British disapproval, the Maroons' social organization prepared them well for success in Sierra Leone. One of the reasons they were able to replace the Nova Scotians in trade was that they used their military units for commercial ventures. The Nova Scotians, with their small-sized, individual efforts, were unable to compete against those of the cohesive Maroons.

Maroon economic ascendency signaled a hiatus in significant female participation in trading. Restricted to farming and petty trade in local markets, Maroon women lacked the necessary mobility for long-distance trading. Despite the sexual freedom that was implied by women's ability to engage in extramarital affairs, women had little economic independence. Unlike many Nova Scotian women who became large-scale property owners, Maroon women accumulated little property on their own. By 1812, fewer than a dozen owned houses. Moreover, inheritance passed to male heads of households and left Maroon women dependent on male family members.[42]

Maroon domination of the intermediary role did not last long, as Liberated African competition soon forced them and even some European merchants out of business. Initially, the arrival after 1807 of the Liberated Africans in Sierra Leone signaled new prosperity for the Nova Scotians and Maroons who were able to capitalize on the need to feed, clothe, and house the Recaptives.[43] Moreover, many Liberated Africans served as apprentices to the Nova Scotians, giving the latter a distinct economic advantage.[44] It cost little to feed and clothe the apprentices, and they provided free labor. The Liberated Africans acculturated rapidly, however, and once freed from their apprenticeships competed with their former masters in the commercial sector.

The British brought the Liberated Africans to Sierra Leone not to be traders but to be farmers. Having blamed the Nova Scotians, rather than the infertile land of the region, for their inattention to farming, the British were similarly disappointed with the Liberated Africans.[45] The Liberated Africans did not ignore farming entirely; produce was grown for both consumption and marketing. Poor transportation, however, interfered with marketing outside of the villages, often restricting sale to the Liberated African Department or in the small village markets.[46]

While women helped men with the farming, they also traded food surpluses such as garden vegetables and fish. Because of poor transportation, women would walk to Freetown carrying their produce on their heads. Although this trade began on an extremely small scale, it provided the basis for a more extensive trade in later years. In Freetown, women as well as men exchanged their produce for merchandise that they took into the interior to exchange for rice. The staple of the Sierra Leonean diet, rice provided a lucrative trade for the Liberated Africans. And they entered the rice trade in large numbers.[47] To increase the scale of their operations some even formed cooperative societies.

The rise of the Liberated Africans marked the reemergence of women in large-scale trading. Walker maintains that the Liberated African women copied the Nova Scotian women's independence from their men, flexible marriage bonds, and zeal for trading. In the face of his positive attempt to address the imbalanced picture of Nova Scotians as mere imitators of British culture, it is unfortunate that he committed a similar error by describing the Liberated Africans as imitators of Nova Scotian society:

> The Nova Scotians exerted "unrelenting cultural pressure on the late arrivals." . . . The logical consequence was that the Liberated African, removed from the source of his own traditional culture, rapidly accepted many aspects of the Nova Scotian alternative and soon became indistinguishable from its originators.[48]

The Liberated Africans were removed physically from their traditional cultures, as were the Nova Scotians; nonetheless they both carried their cultural perspectives with them. If the Recaptives had arrived in Sierra Leone isolated from their countryfolk, perhaps they would have lost much of their cultural heritage. But Liberated Africans were able to join with people from their own ethnic groups. In addition, they shared a common West African heritage. Thus they maintained some cohesion to their past cultures.

This cohesion was facilitated by the large number of Recaptives coming from southern Nigeria. Particularly important among these were Recaptives of Yoruba descent. The large number of Aku, as they were known in Sierra Leone, resulted from the collapse of the Oyo empire, the major Yoruba state, as Yorubaland dissolved into endemic warfare. An upsurge in the slave trade followed in the wake of these struggles.[49] So many Recaptives came from war-racked Yorubaland that a discussion of Yoruba cultural development will illuminate the Liberated African history.

Adherence to Islam distinguished many of the Aku. Some had been Islamized in their homelands during the Fulani jihads of the early nineteenth century. Others were converted in Sierra Leone through contact with the Mandingo and Fula.[50] Despite differences between those Aku who called themselves Muslim and those who professed Christianity, cultural ties gave cohesion to the larger Aku community that transcended religious differences.[51]

One of the Aku culture's prominent features was a predilection for trading. Few contemporary observers overlooked this trait. Writing in 1843, Robert Clarke comments, "The Akoos, who form a great portion of the liberated Africans, are pre-eminently distinguished for their love of trading, and occasionally amass large sums."[52] Aku women traders received special attention in the literature. In 1879, Governor Rowe expressed his admiration for these women.

> The genius of the Sierra Leone people is commercial; from babyhood the Aku girl is a trader, and as she grows up she carries her small wares wherever she can go with safety. The further she goes from the European trading depots the better is her market. . . . These people do more than collect the native produce, they stimulate its cultivation. Many bushels of palm kernels are collected by the native women that they may buy the handkerchief and the looking glass brought to their village by the Sierra Leone adventurers. Had she never visited them, these kernels would have been left to rot on the ground. Tons of colah are exported from Sierra Leone which would never have been fathered from the trees had not this pushing huckster found her way inland. . . . I think I am not exaggerating when I say that nine-tenths of the colah nuts shipped from Sierra Leone are collected by Sierra Leone traders in districts outside the settlement.[53]

Not all the nineteenth-century commentators were European. J. Africanus Horton, the distinguished Sierra Leone doctor and writer, declared that "the [Aku] women make excellent traders, within a very short time they would double, treble, and even quadruple a very small amount."[54]

Aku commercial success can be attributed partly to their Yoruba cultural background and the Sierra Leone setting. Basing its early commerce on the trans-Saharan trade, Yorubaland had long been a center of trade. By the fifteenth century, Oyo had begun to develop into an empire.[55] Not until the early seventeenth century did Oyo begin to take advantage of the Afro-European trade to its south.[56] The empire's wealth was based not only on long-distance trade but also on trade between its numerous small towns and local markets. Indeed, the urbanized setting of Yorubaland laid a fertile ground for trade, since foodstuffs and other essential items had to be provided for craft producers and long-distance traders to free them from agricultural labor.[57] An extensive network of periodic markets evolved to support this trade.[58] Luxury items, imported goods, and fresh meat were largely controlled by men.[59] In some towns, a male secret society, the *Parakoyi,* regulated trade. Among the Egba, for example, this society of "trade chiefs" met every seventeen days to consider the town's trading interests, settle disputes, and regulate prices and standards.[60]

Male control over luxury items reflected the gender hierarchy of the Yoruba. Simi Afonja has argued that

> . . . the unequal structure of trade suggests that the physical presence of women at the market is not a sufficient indicator of their status in the community. The source of wares, the amount of capital imput, and the value of the items for capital accumulation are neglected factors in evaluations of the impact of trade on African women's status.[61]

Moreover, women's services were controlled through a bridewealth system that gave men more access to capital and labor than women.[62] During the nineteenth century, when dependents became increasingly important, one European observer noted that "slaves and wives make a man great in this country."[63]

Women, while they often traveled over long distances pursuing trade, were largely limited to trading in foodstuff and cloth. Their role in the welfare of Oyo's economy was nonetheless considerable. And the sexual division of labor reflected their importance. Men cleared bush, cultivated soil, and harvested palm fruits while women made palm oil, palm kernel oil, soap, and mats for sale domestically and internationally.[64] Throughout the nineteenth century free women increasingly moved away from producing food to concentrating on trade, as towns and cities grew and domestic slaves replaced them on the farms.[65]

The *alafin's* (king's) wealth was based to a large extent on the trading activities of the *ayabas* (king's wives). While many of the alafin's male slaves farmed, his wives, most of whom were really palace slaves, traded this produce along with cloth, natron, and salt.[66] While Hugh Clapperton and Richard Lander were exploring through Oyo they passed parties of up to one hundred women walking to markets.[67] Both palace and other women were freed to travel widely because of their relatively low participation in farming, as compared to most other West African women.

Further, their economic importance was demonstrated by the palace offices that women held. The royal palace in Oyo housed eight titled women of very high rank (including the king's official mother), eight priestesses and dozens of lower level officials (*ilaris*) as well as the ayabas.[68] In addition, each town had an *iyalode* (female chief). Samuel Johnson has provided us with a description of their influence.

> The Iyalode, i.e. the queen of the ladies is a title bestowed upon the most distinguished lady in town. She has also her lieutenant . . . as any of the other principal chiefs of the town. Some of these Iyalodes command a force of powerful warriors, and have a voice in the council of chiefs. Through the Iyalode, the women of the town can make their voices heard in municipal and other affairs.[69]

Although Yoruba women rarely sold luxury items, their custom of traveling long distances to trade prepared them well for the commercial life in Sierra Leone and its hinterland. Certain similarities existed. As in Oyo, women in Sierra Leone took a small part in farming both because men dominated these tasks and because servile labor freed them from farming. In the case of Oyo these servile laborers were slaves; in Sierra Leone they were apprentices.

The Yoruba shared many basic beliefs with the other Recaptives settled in Sierra Leone. Central among these beliefs was the use of the kinship idiom as the ruling ideology.[70] This ideology established a hierarchy based on gender and age, in which each gender was hierarchically structured by age and elders of each gender held authority over younger men and women.[71] Male elders retained more authority than any other sector of the society, as was reflected in their virtual monopoly over the social right to found families. As Paul Lovejoy notes, societies with kinship as the governing principle are characterized by a mode of production based on the lineage structure.[72] This ideology allowed elders to control the labor and reproduction of junior members in societies where land was abundant and labor scarce. In particular, control over women's labor and their reproduction of labor formed a central concern, as women were the principal agricultural workers in most of West Africa. The kinship ideology allowed for polygynous societies in which men exchanged women through marriage.

Yet this was not a stagnant system. The kinship idiom contained a desire for an increasing number of dependents. It was partly in response to this desire that West Africans sought out the Afro-European trade, a commerce that gave increasing numbers the resources to purchase dependents in the form of slaves and wives. The history of the Upper Guinea coast illustrates the changes wrought by this trade. By the eighteenth century, such groups as the Mende, Temne, Vai, and Sherbro were involved so deeply in the transatlantic and domestic slave trades that their own societies were transformed. Most important among these transformations was an increasing stratification of the society into slave versus free peoples.

Slavery had been long-standing in these societies and preceded the international slave trade.[73] Nonetheless, participation in the slave trade led to increased warfare and a consequent increase in the number of slaves held internally. As in many parts of West Africa, women were the preferred slaves because of their importance in agricultural labor and contributions to expanding domestic units.[74] Particularly before the nineteenth century, most slaves were viewed through the kinship idiom. They were not free in that they lacked full kinship rights. Among the Sherbro, slaves lacked the protection of the natal family and had no claims on their offspring; their descendants belonged to their masters.[75] While the slaves' subordinate position was based on the related concepts of nonkin and outsider, domestic slaves became subordinate members of their owners' families. In general they were not sold. Under normal circumstances, the Sherbro addressed slaves using kinship terminology and only during times of stress was a slave's servile status acknowledged.[76]

Not all slaves lived with their masters, however. Over the centuries of Afro-European trade, increasing numbers were settled on slave farms or plantations. The rise of slave villages taxed the kinship ideology that had held West African societies together, as the sheer number of slaves prevented even the appearance that most slaves could become family members. An important function of the ruling kinship ideology began to break down as many slaves could no longer believe that society allowed for their mobility toward free status. By the late eighteenth century the area around the Scarcies rivers witnessed several slave revolts, including a major one at Moriah in which slaves successfully set up a temporary maroon village.[77]

The nineteenth century saw the most dramatic increase in domestic slavery. Cut off from the transatlantic slave trade by the presence of the British, the Upper Guinea coastal peoples used their slaves to produce foodstuffs, kola, and palm products.[78] Among the Mende, Sherbro, and Temne at least half of the population was enslaved, while almost two-thirds of the Vai were slaves—clearly a slave society.[79]

It was during this period of increasing domestic slavery that the Recaptives arrived in Sierra Leone. The trauma of enslavement and resettlement under British control left the Liberated Africans particularly vulnerable to changes in their kinship patterns and the social relations of production. Their colonial masters settled them in villages surrounding Freetown and set about converting them to Christianity. Primary among the attempts at religious "edification" was the British struggle to impose a monogamous marriage structure on Liberated Africans. Some early attempts to obtrude the European marriage institution were laughable. Sent in 1841 to Sierra Leone by the Colonial Office to investigate conditions, Dr. Madden condemned

> . . . the wholesale celebration of the marriage ceremony which formerly took place, when twenty or thirty couples of these people [Liberated Africans] had been marched in one great group

from the Liberated African yard to the Altar to be joined in wedlock, with little previous knowledge of each other, or of the nature of the compact into which they were about to enter. . . . The Assistant Superintendent of the Liberated African Department stated in his replies—viz., that it was a common practice among the newly married people, after a few weeks had elapsed, coming to the magistrates and applying to have their marriage cancelled by mutual consent.[80]

The British notion that husbands should support their wives conflicted with African beliefs. In 1826, the minister of Waterloo Village, outside Freetown, made the following report:

Government has sent to Waterloo since the 24th of June, 56 women who were kept on rations; but no man made application to me to marry any one of them. On the 7th of the present month 30 more were sent to us with an order that they should have rations granted to them for the space of three months only; by which time it was expected that they would be married and be supported by their husbands. I had on this occasion to acquaint the Chief Superintendent that I had no prospect of getting them married in so short a period, the number of single women then kept on rations at the station being 86. On this I received an order from the Hon. Joseph Reffell to send the 30 women just mentioned to Kent, where there are many men in single life who would ere long marry and maintain them. On announcing that the constables of Kent would come to fetch the single women to that station, . . . there arose in the place such a stir for espousals that in the course of two days I had no less than 55 couples on the list to publish the bans of marriage for them on the next Sunday, and on Monday and Tuesday morning couple after couple came forward with applications for marriage, so that when the constables arrived from Kent there were but seven women left for them to carry away. By this means I got them all settled and struck off from rations, but I could clearly perceive that they had formed private connections, and would have been contented to live together in the country fashion without my knowledge, and let Government support the women.[81]

Ten years later, C. B. Jones, the acting superintendent for the Liberated African department, noted the problems with marrying women to men they did not know. Little kept these marriages together. He stated that the department had returned to an old policy of placing women ". . . under the care of respectable married females in order that they may have an opportunity of knowing well the men to whom they are to be united for life."[82]

Nonetheless the British had some successes in spreading their ideas about proper marriage forms among the Recaptives. Along with the missionary attempts, the apprenticeship system, combined with the importance of trading over farming, provided the basis for this partial success. Developed to cope with the large influx of uprooted refugees, the apprenticeship system distributed newly arrived Liberated Africans to more established Sierra Leoneans for up to three years. On the one hand, apprenticeships exposed some new Recaptives to the influence of the monogamous Nova Scotians and, on the other hand, gave men an alternative to plural wives as a source of labor. Many Liberated African women were thus freed from the agricultural tasks for which most West African women were responsible.

In addition, the colony survived more on its trade with the hinterland than on farming.[83] Given the colony's infertile soil, farms that required plural wives were little in evidence, and thus a major economic support for polygyny was lacking.[84] With their free time, Liberated African women put their notions of economic independence to good use in Sierra Leone and followed in the footsteps of the Nova Scotian women. The hiatus in female involvement in trade had ended.

Reflected in flexible marriage bonds, Recaptive men's control over women appears to have diminished. The British insistence that Recaptives give up polygyny for monogamy undercut male control of the marriage institution. Moreover, since the basis for authority over marriage was not firmly entrenched, women appear to have had a great deal of freedom to move in and out of marriage bonds. This freedom contrasted with nineteenth-century Yorubaland, where divorce was rare. According to Samuel Johnson, a Yoruba woman could obtain a divorce if she proved extreme cruelty, but only after vigorous attempts to reconcile husband and wife had failed. Moreover, a divorced woman could not remarry.[85] Testimony of Sierra Leone's more liberal policy was given to the explorer Winwood Reade by a young Mandingo woman who asked to be taken to Freetown "because Sierra Leone was *free*. If a woman did not like her husband, she could leave him and marry another, and there would be no palaver."[86]

While the Sierra Leone experience undermined the marriage structures to which Recaptives had been accustomed, these structures were not completely replaced by the British model. As Fyfe puts it, "If the Freetown people followed conspicuously the Christian precepts of Sabbath-keeping, church going and sobriety, they were less strict in adopting the patriarchal Christian family."[87] Instead, Liberated Africans maintained flexible marriage bonds as their Nova Scotian predecessors had done. These flexible bonds gave both men and women the freedom they needed to travel as far as the Gambia River and Fernando Po in the pursuit of trading ventures.[88]

Most Liberated Africans found themselves parceled out to various villages around the peninsula, some villages having been established especially for them. There the Recaptives began their participation in the Sierra Leone economy by establishing trade within the villages and with Freetown and its hinterland. Seaside villages such as Kent and York developed a flourishing trade in fish, a product that could be sold in Freetown as well as in the interior. York farmers also produced cassava, ginger, cocoa yams, and potatoes, which the traders combined with *fufu* and *gari* to sell in Freetown and Waterloo.[89]

Three miles from Freetown, Kissy village evolved into an important market town. According to Robert Clarke, senior assistant surgeon, the Aku and Igbo predominated among Kissy's Liberated African settlers.[90] Most farmed, raising yams, sweet potatoes, cassava, maize, cocoa, peppers, and several varieties of legumes.[91] Along with the rice and palm products purchased from the Temne, Susu, Mandingo, and Bullom peoples, these goods could be disposed of by the women at the village open market or carried to Freetown.[92]

Mountain villages became known for their garden vegetables. Lettuce, radishes, parsley, onions, and tomatoes were raised at Leicester and Regent and transported daily to the Freetown market. Head porterage was the only means of transporting goods to Freetown, and as each carrier was limited to about a bushel and a half of produce, trading was a difficult occupation.[93]

The Freetown Traders

By the 1830s, the village people began to settle permanently in Freetown. Pursuing various domestic trades as well as marketing, women found the conveniences of Freetown inviting. Indeed, with its polyglot population, Freetown offered many opportunities for commercial success. As a growing central marketing area it attracted many to its local markets. Caravan traders, settled strangers, ship crews, all had to be provided with foodstuffs. Liberated African women hustled to exploit these opportunities.

These acquisitive women competed successfully in the meat trade. Betsy Carew, a Hausa Recaptive, utilized contacts built up by her husband Thomas, a Bambara-born butcher. Together they took over the army contract from Macaulay and Babington, a major British owned company, when it collapsed. They also acted as landlords to cattle caravans coming from the interior.[94] During the 1830s and 1840s, Betsy Carew was at her greatest prominence. A. B. C. Sibthorpe, the Liberated African historian, claimed that she was known and respected by every European merchant in the colony. Her transactions with them were substantial. One merchant advanced her three thousand pounds' worth of goods, and within two months she was able to reduce her bill to nineteen hundred pounds.[95] Carew captured the attention of Mary Church, wife of a British colonial officer, who commented on her dignified carriage and elaborate dress style. Church found it curious that Carew would appear to be more important than her husband Thomas in their joint business ventures.[96] In fact, the husband was a substantial property owner in his own right.[97] Indicative of their social standing was the marriage of their British-educated daughter Hannah to one of the most successful second-generation Maroons, Joseph Green Spilsbury.[98] Yet despite this sign of social acceptance, the Carews ended their lives in debt.[99]

Elizabeth Coles competed with Carew for the meat trade. Although it is unclear where Coles was born, Butt-Thompson claims she arrived in Sierra Leone about 1827. Beginning her stay as an apprentice to the Carrols, a family of Nova Scotian women who owned a farm near Waterloo, Coles went on to become Syble Boyle's housekeeper.[100] It was convenient for Coles to end up in Boyle's house, as he was a leading Aku merchant. From a shop on Water Street he sold locally produced wares. In 1872, Governor Kennedy appointed Boyle to a permanent seat as an unofficial representative on the legislative council.[101] The house where Coles worked has been described by Christopher Fyfe:

> Syble Boyle's house in Trelawney Street displayed the standard he and his friends aspired to. Its pedimented windows, iron-work balconies, pillared upstairs drawing-room with a bust of Queen Victoria and a large gilt mirror over the fireplace, imitated the kind of house being built in rich bourgeois quarters in Europe. There he could entertain the Colonial Secretary or the leading European businessmen in the sort of surroundings they aspired to themselves.[102]

Gaining Boyle's trust and assistance, Coles took advantage of her new setting. She teamed up with Cornelius Crowther, a wealthy Waterloo merchant, to become a provisioner to the garrison and to naval ships. Eventually she bought the Carrol farm where she had served as an apprentice.[103]

Betsy Carew and Elizabeth Coles stand out in their success, for most Sierra Leone women traders operated on a much smaller scale. Clustered around Little East Street, many of these traders spread their wares out on the ground. The more successful, such as Harriet Willis Benjamins of 10 Little East Street, had small shops. This was a particularly good area for petty trading, as women were exposed to the waterborne traffic from Big, Suppit, and King Jimmy wharfs. Little East Street even attracted some of the biggest settler men traders such as Malama Thomas, Walter Nicol, and John Willis Benjamins.[104]

The Big Market

Many other of Freetown's businesswomen found trading in marketplaces both convenient and lucrative. And they often banded together to protect their economic interests. As early as 1850, the market traders complained about Freetown's inadequate and deteriorating markets and forced the government to recognize that the market's "deplorable state of disrepair" needed to be addressed if market dues were to be collected justifiably "from the inhabitants resorting to Buildings in which it is impossible to remain during the Rains."[105] Pressure from these traders resulted in the construction of the Vegetable Market, commonly called the Big Market.[106] In 1861, Governor Steven Hill proudly reported the previous year's completion of

> . . . our new market house . . . affording advantages which are duly appreciated. It is a substantial stone building, roofed with slate, and having an extensive skylight for ventilation. Its length is 240 feet and its breadth 60 feet."[107]

The early history of the Big Market demonstrates the crucial need that the market successfully fulfilled. Further, the market's history parallels the history of Sierra Leonean women traders. The competition to obtain one of the limited number of selling spaces required more than mere luck and one day's stall fee; thus the Big Market attracted already successful traders. As Governor Steven Hill pointed out, in its first year the Big Market had become overcrowded. "Although commodious, it is found insufficient for the multitude of people resorting to it, many of whom have to take their position for selling outside."[108] Successful traders rented space by the month as they realized the importance of establishing an identifiable spot in the market. Among the earliest vendors were sisters Jane Mends and Mary Powells, two of the first female ship chandlers in Freetown and aunts of Abi Jones.[109] They provided the foundation of a business that thrived into the 1970s as Jones Brothers of King Jimmy.

Two years after the Big Market was built, Richard Burton passed through Freetown and published his useful but racist account of life there. Included in this account is a description of the Big Market.

> . . . the neat building with blind arches and flying roof. Externally stone and internally brick, this bazaar has half its floor paved and other half expecting to be. . . . The market—it contained tai-

lors—was full of fat middle-aged negresses, sitting at squat before their "blies" or round baskets, which contained a variety and
confusion of heterogeneous articles, of which the following is a
list as disorderly as the collection which it enumerates. There
were pins and needles, yarn and thread . . . needle-cases, with all
kinds of hardware, looking glasses in lacquered frames, beads of
sorts, cowries and achatinae . . . poor and cheap ginger, . . . dried
bats and rats, . . . reels of cotton, kolas, . . . and sheabutter nuts,
country snuff-boxes of a chestnut-like nut, . . . bluestone, col-
cohtan, and other drugs, physic nuts, . . . shallots, dried peppers,
red and black; horns of goat and antelope, smoked and dried
fish, . . . groundnut, very poor rice, and feathers of a plantain
bird. To the walls were suspended dry goods, red woolen night-
caps and comforters, leopard and monkey skins, and the spoils of
an animal that might have been a gazelle.[110]

In addition, Burton described the various fruits, such as limes,
bananas, and avocados, and the vegetables, such as okra, eggplant,
and yams, also found on sale.[111]

The sense one gets from Burton's account is of a lively, thriving
marketplace crammed with vendors and their wares. Twenty-five
years later, the market was as lively as ever. A British civil servant
who served in Freetown, G. A. Lethbridge Banbury, declared that
on busy days the Big Market was louder than the tower of Babel.
Although the police were seldom required to enforce order, the
furor was so great that ". . . a stranger would believe that a never-
ending battle of arms and tongues is proceeding."[112]

Freetown's expanding economy easily accommodated the Big
Market. Allen Howard has pointed out that in terms of the central
place theory articulated by Walter Christaller and A. Losch, Freetown was the single highest order place in Sierra Leone and its
hinterland.[113] In the market hierarchy, the Big Market served as a
central market in Freetown's economy. Indeed, its location was
strategic. Down by the main wharf, near the customs house and
other important government buildings, stood the new marketplace. The wharf known as Government Wharf determined the
main commercial and business areas, for in the days before rail-
roads and automobiles trade depended heavily on waterborne
transport. Thus Government Wharf was at the center of Sierra

Leone's transportation network. Every Tuesday, Thursday, and Saturday farmers and intermediaries arrived there from Bullom shores with their goods for sale at King Jimmy Market. Despite Freetown's natural deep-water harbor, which allowed big ships to sail in freely, Susan's Bay provided these traders with the shelter they needed to land their small craft at Freetown.[114]

European merchants found the Big Market, located in the central business district, convenient. Big Market traders competed successfully for the business of supplying the many ships that anchored at the Freetown port. In exchange for these provisions, merchants provided Big Market traders with imported goods, and so the imports began their downward journey in Sierra Leone's marketing hierarchy.

Location in the central business district had further advantages. Along with other colony-born traders, the women of the Big Market took advantage of the discount sales of impounded goods sold at the customs house situated behind the marketplace. In addition, the women profited by proximity to other government institutions that clustered around Government Wharf. For example, provisions for the government hospital and police station came from the Big Market.[115] Since traders also provided retailing services, the Big Market's location near government offices provided further advantages; the Europeans found the market the most convenient place to shop for many necessities in one stop.

In its strategic location the Big Market, easily fulfilling the functions of a central market, connected the local, national, and international economies. Goods destined for each level could be found there. At the local level, goods were exchanged on a retail basis. Among these goods were the vegetables and crafts purchased from Bullom farmers and intermediaries. Largely destined for local consumption, these vegetables included rice, peppers, corn, and palm oil, as well as the various leaves, such as cassava, potato, and *crin-crin*, so prominent in Sierra Leonean food. The Bullom producers and traders were not the only traders who sold vegetables to the Big Market vendors, however. Women from the peninsula villages brought their goods to market as well. These goods reflected the various specializations of the villages. Twice a week, Liberated African women from seaside villages such as York brought cassava, potato leaves, ginger, cocoa yams, fufu, gari, and farina.[116] From mountain villages such as Leicester, Recaptive women brought their garden vegetables. In addition to these items, which both men and women grew, the mountain village women supplied the Big Market vendors with fruits. Because of the proximity of the mountain villages to Freetown, some women would travel to the Big Market daily.[117] A few obtained their own stalls there.[118]

Thus on a daily basis the Big Market provided local produce and cottage goods to Freetown's population. Generally, the consumers of these retailed items were European and African elites who enjoyed the convenience of shopping in the covered market. Along with this retail function went the prestige the traders gained from serving European customers.

But more lucrative for the Big Market traders was trading on the national level. This operation involved important bulking functions. From various markets about town, Big Market vendors purchased goods, bulked them, and prepared them for transport to the peninsula villages. In addition, some items (onions, for example) found their way further into the interior. The same traders who bought the Big Market vegetables took these bulked goods back to their villages for sale.

In addition to bulking produce in preparation for the domestic trade, Big Market traders bulked produce for export. This produce flowed in the opposite direction from other central place markets. Principal among these goods were palm products and kola nuts. By assisting in this outward flow of commodities into the international economy, the Big Market helped pull the Freetown hinterland into the wider economy.

As they helped with the upward flow of commodities, so too they aided with the downward flow. For this task they provided bulk-breaking services. In exchange for produce European firms supplied traders with imported manufactured goods. This exchange was based on a credit system in which the European firms advanced goods to the marketwomen.[119] Thus Big Market vendors endeavored to build up good credit relations with European firms in order to be assured of a steady supply of imported goods. To establish credit, the women attempted to develop a close relationship with at least one firm employee, whom they called a "special customer." Sometimes the basis for this relationship lay in the Big Market itself, where vendors sought to impress European customers with their business acumen. At other times women came to know European employees by supplying other services, such as laundering, and subsequently asking to be advanced goods based on the trust established in this nontrading transaction. Finally, women asked relatives to intercede for them to guarantee their creditworthiness. These relatives were often women who had already established themselves with a firm; but the intermediary could also be a male relative who had economic dealings with the firm.[120]

Most of the purchases made by individual Big Market traders were small, rarely over ten pounds. Some women joined together to make larger purchases, but even these transactions seldom exceeded fifty pounds.[121] Fortunately, in Sierra Leone's economy purchases valued at ten pounds were more than sufficient for entering trade.

The Big Market also had extraeconomic functions, for it served as a center of interethnic contact and as a channel of communication between ethnic groups. In Sierra Leone, the Big Market stood like a central clearinghouse, assimilating and adapting European culture and diffusing it throughout the hinterland via its trading networks. Alternately, it assimilated and adapted indigenous culture and spread it throughout the various ethnic groups and to the European community. Thus the traders aided in the development of a supraethnic culture that today can be identified as Sierra Leonean. For example, Big Market traders brought together local manufacturers, clothing styles, and processed food from all over Sierra Leone and even from other territories such as Guinea, Liberia, and The Gambia. Moreover, the "special customer" relationships, semipermanent credit ties that Big Market traders established both up and down the economic hierarchy, served as interethnic channels of communication.

For example, Big Market traders were instrumental in passing along information about medicines, as the market vendors learned the different herbal medicines from various ethnic groups around Sierra Leone. Although the traders were primarily Liberated Africans, they dispensed the medicine of the Susu, Mende, Temne, and other local groups as well as the herbs of the homeland of the Recaptive (Yoruba, Igbo, or Hausa). Thus they helped establish a pharmacology that was common to all of Sierra Leone.[122] In addition, customers in the Big Market could be introduced to cottage goods from around Sierra Leone. A Mende could buy a Susu-made basket, or an Aku could purchase a Mandingo-made charm.[123]

While Big Market traders acted as an integrative force between ethnic groups, they also helped integrate the diverse elements of Liberated African society into a cohesive ethnic group. In the Big Market, the most successful Yoruba women met the most successful Igbo and Popo and Temne traders. Here, as they banded together for mutual economic gains, their identification as Big Market traders began to supercede their identification as Yoruba, Igbo, Popo, or Temne. Moreover, certain traders, such as Abi Jones, a well-known trader, became models whom other Big Market women followed. And as visible and successful women, these traders served as models of behavior for those Sierra Leonean women outside of the market who aspired to economic success. Other institutions, such as churches and schools, served as a focus for cultural integration within colony society; these institutions have been discussed by others.[124] The role of the marketplace as a central place for communication and for cultural and normative exchange within Sierra Leonean society has been ignored. As the preeminent market, the Big Market stood in the center of this communication and cultural exchange network.

Big Market traders formed an important core in Krio society. Other colony women observed their behavior closely, and they went to the marketplace to learn the gossip and important news events. In the marketplace women with diverse origins (i.e., Igbo and Hausa) and from different locations (i.e., Leicester Village and Freetown) joined together and developed opinions that others respected and that became part of the group consensus.

The Kola Trade and the Sierra Leone Women's Diaspora

While many women, like the Big Market vendors, based their trade in Freetown, many others went up the surrounding rivers to establish themselves. Few of these traders had transactions worth more than £100 at a time. Nonetheless, roaming as far as Fernando Po and the Senegambia region, they took their goods into the hinterland to exchange for rice, palm products, groundnuts, and kola.[125] Their participation in the kola trade grew from the mid-nineteenth century to be extensive and substantial. A focus on this trade may help to elucidate the Sierra Leone women's role in the growth of the colony's economy.

The kola trade from Sierra Leone has a long history, going back at least four centuries to the mid-1500s. From this early period, Sierra Leone became a major exporter to the Senegambia and the upper Niger river regions. Fortunately, Sierra Leone was blessed with *nitida*, a type of kola that was highly valued in the savanna. The most ancient of the trade routes by which kola traveled were overland. The kola trade was part of a larger exchange between the forest and the Sudan that included iron, salt, palm oil, gold, and slaves.[126] The expansion of trade in the Sudan from the sixteenth century, consequent upon the spread of Fula and Mande settlements, led to an increase in the kola trade. Further expansions in the trade were influenced by developments in the eighteenth century, including the establishment of Futa Jallon.

The older, overland trade was rivaled by a coastal trade dominated by Portuguese and Afro-Portuguese traders. As Allen Howard suggests, the participation of the Portuguese in this trade dispels the myth that kola has been a purely African trade. These Europeans and Afro-Europeans continued in this coastal trade well into the late 1800s.[127]

Expanding demand brought on by the growth of the new Islamic states to the north benefited both the overland and coastal trades. The rising standard of living in the north and the growing Muslim population that used kola as its only stimulant contributed to a marked increase in the kola trade with the savanna.[128]

As early as the 1850s, Sierra Leoneans had become heavily committed to the kola trade.[129] Spreading out from Lagos to Senegambia, the Sierra Leoneans positioned themselves to take a leading role. While both men and women took part in the trade and some of the men became big traders, Sierra Leonean women were more numerous.[130] By the late nineteenth century, women were most closely identified with the trade.[131]

A small portion of the kola exported by the Sierra Leonean women went down the coast to Nigeria. Using their contacts with the Yoruba Saro (Liberated Africans who had returned to their Yoruba homeland) the Sierra Leoneans were able to cash in on the market up the Niger River in present-day northern Nigeria.[132] It is

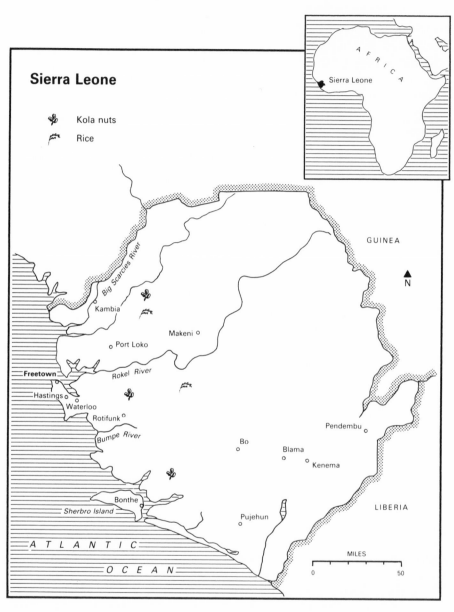

Map 1. Sources of Kola and Rice Trade before 1898. (Adapted from John I. Clarke, ed., *Sierra Leone in Maps* [London, 1966], pp. 17, 75.)

difficult to determine the extent of female participation at this early stage; it is even possible that the trade was dominated by men. Babatunde Agiri, in his discussion of the role of the Yoruba Saro in introducing nitida kola to Nigeria, mentions only men. By the 1800s the trading diaspora from Sierra Leone to Nigeria had lost control of the trade to Hausa traders.[133]

Of more long-term importance to the Sierra Leonean kola merchants was the trade up the coast to Guinea-Bissau, The Gambia, and Senegal. Their entrance into the trade led to the expansion of the coastal trade until then dominated by the Portuguese and Afro-Portuguese. Sierra Leonean women traders were well placed to take advantage of this trade. Small concentrations of these women could be found throughout the Scarcies River area of northern Sierra Leone in what the British came to call Karene District. According to British trade reports, between 1895 and 1899 colony women who traded in kola could be found in Kambia, Samu, Magbeli, Port Loko, Mambolo, and Sande Loko. Some reports listed only Karene District. Other women could be found in Mabang, Kwia, and Romangay. While the kola trade was important to these women, few, if any, specialized in kola alone, as they also traded for palm products, rice, benne (sesame) seed, and rubber. Food exchanged for these products included rum, gin, cotton goods, tobacco, salt, beads, and occasionally cash.[134]

The center of the Sierra Leonean women's kola trade lay to the south on Sherbro Island. It was on the basis of observations on Sherbro Island that District Commissioner Joshua T. Alldridge claimed that the kola nut trade was entirely in the hands of the Sierra Leonean women. Situated at the base of several riverine routes, Sherbro Island traders captured much of the area's produce trade. In addition, taking advantage of the island's relatively deep harbor, traders often bypassed Freetown and shipped directly to other ports in Africa or to Europe. Only after improvements were made to Freetown's harbor in the late nineteenth century did Sherbro lose its competitive stance in the export trade.

Before large-scale contact with the Sierra Leone colony, no specialized trading had evolved in the Mende country surrounding the Sherbro hinterland from which these kola were drawn, and internal marketing was undeveloped. While long-distance trade routes crossed Mende country and connected it with the rest of West

Africa, trade between towns was on a small scale; no periodic markets existed.[135]

The Sherbro and its hinterland's economy was well suited for
the largely small-scale traders coming from Freetown as early as
the 1790s. The earliest traders came to Sherbro searching for rice
to supply Freetown's growing population. After the establishment
of the American Mende Mission in the 1840s, the island's settler
population grew steadily.[136] By the late 1850s, the Sherbro had
become economically important to the colony, which led Britain to
annex it to Sierra Leone in 1861.[137] Afterward, the commerce at
the administrative town of Bonthe became so brisk that Alldridge
described the town as "essentially a trading place . . . [where] every-
body who is not a government official or a minister of religion is
engaged in trade of some kind."[138] Indeed, even many government officials and missionaries engaged in trade. Besides the kola
nuts, important produce trade included rice, palm oil, and palm
kernels.

During the kola harvest season (from September to just before
Christmas) the kola trade dominated the attention of the Sierra
Leone women traders.[139] Their exodus from Bonthe into the
rivers visibly affected the town's population.[140] During the early
years of the trade, some of the kola collected was shipped directly
to Senegambia, Guinea-Bissau, and Nigeria; but by the end of the
1890s most kola was diverted through Freetown.

The colonial government's annual reports for the 1890s give
some idea how extensive the Sierra Leonean kola trade had grown
by the end of the century. Although growth was not continuous,
the value of kola exports grew from £40,866 in 1895 to £61,645 in
1899 (table 1). Reaching a zenith of 12,716 hundredweight in 1897,
just before the 1898 war caused a precipitous drop in exports, the
increased value and volume reflected a growing demand in The
Gambia. Almost half (4,710 hundredweight) of the kola nuts exported were shipped to The Gambia in 1899.[141]

In the second half of the nineteenth century, Liberated African
women from both The Gambia and Sierra Leone used cheap
steamship passage to carry their kola and other goods to Bathurst,
The Gambia. From there they spread out through Senegambia to
sell their goods. Muslim Krios from Foulah Town and Fourah Bay
in Freetown were particularly prominent in this trade.[142] In the

1860s, kola by the basket cost from eight to eleven pounds in Sierra
Leone and could be sold from eighteen to twenty pounds at Mac-
Carthy Island, The Gambia.[143] The high profits from this trade
enriched the Liberated African community in Senegambia. Florence Mahoney notes that "by the late eighties, profits from kola
were being made available for imports of manufactured goods
direct from Manchester and Liverpool; and it was by such means
that Africans came to participate in the groundnut trade as merchants in their own right."[144]

The Sierra Leonean women organized their participation in the
trade by forming a trading diaspora. The connection between
Freetown and Senegambia was one important aim of this network.
Commercial diasporas facilitated trade between ethnic groups and,
before the development of the world capitalist system, these diasporas conducted most interethnic trade. While they appeared
distinct from their host cultures, members of these diasporas famil-
iarized themselves with customs in various cultures and thus acted
as brokers between the cultures.[145] First, diasporas established networks of traders whose ties allowed for the development of trust
and credit. Second, the networks eased communication about
prices and trading conditions. Third, the networks enabled groups
to establish authority and order over trade routes.[146]

Although the Sierra Leonean women were flexible enough to
absorb noncolony women into their diaspora, they established a
distinctive look that made them identifiable as a trading network.

TABLE 1.   Kola Nut Exports, 1895–99

Year	Volume (in cwt.)	Value (in £)
1895	9,927	40,866
1896	9,712	38,352
1897	12,716	46,552
1898	10,795	49,671
1899	9,619	61,645

Source: *Annual Report for Sierra Leone, 1899*
(Freetown: Sierra Leone Government), p. 24.

Alldridge has provided us with a description of these Sierra Leone traders that sounds remarkably like the dress of the older Krio woman trader today. "They generally appear in a starched print gown. . . . A bright Madras handkerchief for the head is indispensible; it is tied with great art, with its two ends standing up stiffly in front."[147]

Perhaps the most distinctive characteristic of the network was the Sierra Leonean women's connections to the colony. They moved about with a sense of independence unusual for women in the Sierra Leone hinterland. Moreover, many women professed belief in Christianity or Islam and thus became involved in religions that aided their adaptation to a trading life-style. Yet while colony connections and membership in a universal religion helped to distinguish the women traders from other women, these were relatively loose membership criteria. Because of the large influx of Liberated Africans from many parts of Western Africa and the steady increase in the population from the hinterland, ethnic boundaries in nineteenth-century Sierra Leone were flexible. Colony connections, therefore, could be manufactured or developed. The Muslim Sierra Leone women shared Islam with many other women in the area. And missionaries eagerly spread the tenets of Christianity to any who showed interest. Thus the religion of the traders presented little barrier to participation by other women. In addition, the Sierra Leoneans possessed neither identifying facial marks nor an exclusive language, for their facial marks stemmed from a variety of ethnic groups found throughout West Africa, and Krio evolved as a trading language that many understood.

As Philip Curtin suggests, trade diasporas evolved because of a need for brokers ". . . who understood the different ways of life of disparate trade partners as well as the intricacies of the market."[148] The Sierra Leonean women traders acted as cultural and economic brokers by familiarizing themselves with both European and indigenous cultures. This dual understanding is revealed by a closer look at their eclectic cosmology: many women combined Christianity or Islam with African religious beliefs that had their roots in indigenous cultures and the home cultures of the Liberated Africans.

Christianity connected them with Europeans and Liberated African groups in Senegambia. Islam was also an important connection between the Aku of Sierra Leone and The Gambia. Other writers have tended to overemphasize the extent of Westernization among nineteenth-century Sierra Leoneans and thus their closeness to the European traders.[149] It is true, however, that the shared experience of Christian conversion helped bind together a very loose-knit trading diaspora. For many kola traders based on Sherbro Island, Christianity clearly performed this function. Before leaving Bonthe for the rivers at the beginning of the kola harvest season, the women would gather in churches to pray for success.[150] In the face of the intense competition to follow, this community experience lent some cohesion to the group. Women who moved to Bathurst could attend churches and thus be exposed to other women with whom they could form alliances. In this way the Liberated Africans' diaspora was further cemented.

John Peterson's excellent work on Liberated African society underscores the continuing importance of "prior systems of African beliefs" among the Liberated Africans.[151] For example, he suggests that after making offers to their gods the Aku used kola nuts to divine the gods' reactions. During a smallpox epidemic at Fourah Bay in 1859, kola nuts were used to uncover its cause. In addition, other ties to the past, such as secret societies of Yoruba origin, persisted.[152]

Indigenous systems of beliefs, because they evolved within the context of life in the Upper Guinea coast, also played a major role in Sierra Leonean women's lives. Bundu, for example, began spreading among the Liberated Africans at least by the late 1850s. An 1858 smallpox epidemic created an impetus for women of Hastings and Wellington to join, as Bundu women held a well-deserved reputation as medical specialists.[153] From Hastings, Bundu spread throughout the peninsula. Muslim Krios particularly found Bundu attractive; many insisted that potential wives graduate first from the "Bundu bush."[154] By the 1880s, important segments of the colony population considered Bundu a threat to the colony's moral fiber.[155] Membership in Bundu brought the women closer to indigenous women and thus facilitated trade between them. As cultural brokers, therefore, the Sierra Leonean women used Bundu as an entrée into indigenous society.

Among the Vai, Gola, Kirm, and most importantly for the kola traders, the Sherbro, Bundu/Sande seem to have existed for centuries. Influenced by Madame Yoko, the powerful Mende chief who established a chapter at Moyamba, the Mende began adopting it during the nineteenth century. Madame Yoko used the society to make alliances by taking girls into the Bundu bush, treating them as wards, and finding them husbands.[156] Bundu, as well as the men's secret society, Poro, became increasingly important for the Mende as they confronted the unstable political atmosphere of the nineteenth-century Upper Guinea coast. Slave raiding and warfare brought war chiefs to the forefront of political power. The Mende search for institutions to mediate the new authority established by the war chiefs led to the adoption of the secret societies. The societies represented the interests of the ancestors: that is, the interests of the corporate bodies of men and women. Bundu and Poro could sanction those secular authorities for offending the ancestors and thus counterbalance their power. Moreover, the societies promoted cohesion and developed a sense of group purpose that allowed various Mende groups to establish claims over land and control over people's labor.[157]

Paradoxically, Bundu represented both female solidarity and intragroup antagonism. The solidarity grew out of the initiation experience. Girls tended to join their mothers' chapters, where they were certified and prepared for marriage. Throughout a woman's life she would maintain ties to her original chapter as she returned to her natal village to give birth, to participate in important ceremonies, and if she wished to "retire" during her later years. But she also joined the Bundu chapter in her husband's village where she moved after marriage.[158] Thus she became linked to the women born in that village as well as to the other wives who had married into the family. By connecting her to women in similar positions, membership in Bundu modified the isolation a young wife might feel when she moved to her husband's village. By belonging to societies in both their natal and husbands' villages, women extended their political and social networks throughout the region. The possibilities for the free flow of information between societies on issues that affected women in the area were heightened by this bonding between women in different Bundu chapters.[159]

In the interest of women as a whole, Bundu protected women from overly abusive husbands and inappropriate male sexual behavior.[160] Moreover, the head of each chapter represented women's interests to men through their control over an important Poro office. Women were thus present at all deliberations that affected women's lives.[161] Yet Bundu chapters were hierarchical in structure and represented the interests of older women more strongly than younger women. This antagonism between older and younger women was symbolized by the initiation rite of clitoridectomy, a practice that contributed to the control of women's sexuality. Male elders clearly benefited from this attempt to gain control over younger women's sexuality and, by extension, their labor. But older women also benefited from control over younger women's sexuality, for they arranged marriages, extracted initiation fees from men, and brought junior wives into their husbands' families. Older women gained from the labor of these women, also, as they looked for ways to escape the arduous farming life that most women faced.

Bundu, then, helped older women control younger women's labor and sexuality. Nonetheless it did help create cohesion among all women. As Janet Bujra argues, in exogamous, virilocal societies, ". . . solidarity is a genuinely political act in which women overcome the division between them in a wider realization of their common situation *vis-à-vis* men."[162] Thus at the same time that Bundu represented older women's interests more than those of younger women, it also demonstrated a feminist character by insuring solidarity among women and representing the interests of the women's community as a whole to men.

Joining Bundu was of particular significance for Liberated African women in their attempts to cement ties with indigenous women. Those who joined Bundu gained some of the protection they forfeited by traveling about without the protection of their families. Membership in secret societies and religious organizations also set moral standards by which Sierra Leonean women felt constrained to lead their lives. Women traders, sharing religious and cultural experiences, laid a foundation on which to base trust. And in an economy in which contractual relations had to be based on personal knowledge of the people involved, establishing a basis for trust was essential.

The intimateness of the Sierra Leone diaspora helped establish criteria for developing contractual relations. Traders could ill afford to advance goods to untrustworthy agents. Although the size of transactions was often small, the hazards were great. Threats of kidnapping, robbery, and illness combined to present agents with many obstacles to meeting their credit obligations. Thus traders attempted to minimize risks by extending credit to those whom they felt they could trust, and these trusted individuals were usually either relatives or connected in the diaspora through one of the various organizations. Finally, membership in secret societies and other organizations provided the basis for authority. By establishing a hierarchy of women, traders were obligated to adhere to the decisions made by women in the upper reaches of the societies. Thus women's activities were effectively regulated and monitored.

While nineteenth-century conflict between Sierra Leoneans and indigenous people has been overemphasized (reflecting present-day more than past conditions),[163] trading did have its dangers for colony women. The possibility of kidnapping and enslavement did exist since domestic slavery was still widely practiced. Yet the most common hazard was robbery. For example, based at Kambia, Annie Wilson traded in rice, rubber, boards, and kola nuts and obtained these goods in exchange for cotton goods, tobacco, salt, and rum.[164] In 1894 she complained to James Parkes, the secretary of native affairs, that goods worth £9.17.0 had been stolen from her and that she had received no cooperation from the alikali of Kambia. Parkes wrote Alikali Koya Bubu, reporting her complaint and asking for assistance in recovering her goods.[165] As of January 2, 1895, Parkes had received no favorable response from the alikali and thus threatened to deduct the compensation from Bubu's stipend.[166] Unfortunately, the final resolution of the dispute does not appear in the archival record.

While the incidents of looting and enslavement of Sierra Leonean traders should not be overemphasized, such incidents point to the problem of stranger-traders in the hinterland societies. Sierra Leoneans became important to the growth of the hinterland economies, yet as outsiders they sometimes caused resentment.[167] As George Simmel has argued, strangers, because of their ambiguous positions, are often targeted as scapegoats during periods of unrest.[168] Building on Simmel, Shack notes that settled strangers, "being betwixt and between, neither alien nor citizen," become identified with deep-rooted social problems.[169] Several Africanist scholars have addressed the change in stranger-host relations that occurred with the imposition of colonial rule.[170] They argue that colonial rule changed the status of strangers within African societies both by forcing societies to accept unwanted strangers and by undermining traditional constraints on all strangers. The historical relationship of subordination-superordination between strangers and hosts was disrupted. Now strangers were to be treated as equals.[171]

These writers err, however, in overemphasizing the discontinuity between stranger-host relations in the pre-colonial and colonial eras. The Sierra Leone material indicates that the colony exercised some controls over stranger-host relations long before the imposition of colonial rule. When stranger-traders were looted and felt themselves unable to receive fair justice from the local authorities, they turned to Freetown. By carefully manipulating the system of stipends and by implied threats of force, colonial officials attempted to protect the traders' interests.[172] Thus interior rulers were forced to respect the traders' rights and even to allow some unwanted strangers to operate unharmed in their midst. Formal colonial rule represented a shift towards more control rather than a change from a total lack of control.

In 1869 Sarah Fox, a trader on the Small Scarcies River, wrote to the governor:

It appears that some evil disposed person yet unknown must have set the factory on fire for the purpose of plundering, which has been proved by the conduct of one Kehbly a notorious marauder and companion of Cafee; he with a band of his men and other native residents of the place under the pretext of assisting to extinguishing the fire broke open the doors of my store which were fireproof and plunder a large amount of goods and produce amounting to the sum of one thousand dollars, all application and entreaties for the restoration of the things plundered was in vain, excepting two barrels of rum.

Knowing no other method to adopt but to appeal to your Excellency I therefore must respectfully beg to request your Excellency's interference in the matter which I am sure will be of immense help to me in recovering at least some portion of my property.[173]

The governor passed this letter on to the government inter-preter, Thomas George Lawson, who handled most affairs with the rulers from the hinterland. Lawson sent a representative, Robert Davis, to the ruler in the area, Bey Ingar.[174] Davis confirmed that Fox had been robbed by Kehbly and his men under the pretense of extinguishing a fire that they themselves had set. Bey Ingar and Bey Bureh, the chief of the territory where Kehbly resided, agreed to help gain restitution for Sarah Fox's property.

This example illustrates two further points. First, precolonial strangers were not lone individuals selfishly trading only for their own profit. In fact many strangers collectively represented the in-terests of their homeland or at least maintained ties with one or two particular places. Many trading strangers formed part of commer-cial diasporas and thus should be seen as intermediaries between cultures, facilitating commerce and cultural contact.[175] As repre-sentatives of a diaspora, many strangers had external authorities to whom they could turn to support their interests, whether these authorities were colonial rulers in Freetown or Malian officials in Timbuktu. Given that trading diasporas formed the basis of most long-distance African trade, few rulers took lightly disruption of this trade through the ill-treatment of strangers. Indeed, many strangers who became powerful within their hosts' communities demonstrated not only their own personal charisma and attraction but also the power and influence of their homeland on the internal affairs of the host societies.

Second, the establishment of colonial rule was a long, drawnout process that included a period of expanding informal colonial rule. The Sierra Leonean women helped ease the evolution of colonial rule by establishing themselves as settled strangers in the interior and thus not only acting as agents for the transfer of goods but also cementing the political ties between the hinterland and the colony.

The colony's strangers nevertheless created concern for local authorities. As Elliot Skinner suggests, strangers are often suspect and deemed dangerous because they sometimes ignore or misin-terpret social norms.[176] This was certainly true for Sierra Leone's women traders. By living outside of wedlock and trading indepen-dently, they greatly deviated from the norms of indigenous society. These female strangers offered a special challenge to the ruling elite, for they stood as a model of the possibilities of an independent life-style. Evidence exists that women seeking to escape their traditional roles adapted to this life-style by joining the Sierra Leonean women's network.[177] Such renegade women directly threatened the agriculturally based economies by enticing away their labor force. Thus the existence of this alternative life-style threatened male control of women's labor.

While Sierra Leonean women were vulnerable to attacks from hosts uncomfortable with their trading practices and life-style, other problems threatened their prosperity even more. As actors on the periphery of the world economy, these women had little control over the economic forces that determined much of their success. And in the late nineteenth century the economic picture was ominous.

Prices for African produce fell rapidly while prices for imported goods fell only slightly and gradually. The price of Sierra Leone's most important export, palm oil, fell almost 50 percent in the twenty-nine-year period from 1861–65 to 1886–90. While prices averaged thirty-seven pounds per ton in the former period, prices dropped to twenty pounds per ton in the latter. Similarly, palm kernel prices fell almost a third between the 1860s and the mid-1880s: from fifteen pounds per ton to ten pounds per ton.[178] Prices fell for two main reasons. First, the discovery of oil in the United States during the 1860s and the 1869 opening of the Suez Canal (through which Indian groundnuts and Australian tallow could now flow) made West African palm produce less valuable. Second, the European demand for oils and fats dropped because Europe was in the midst of a mild economic crisis.[179]

African intermediaries in the European coastal enclaves were particularly affected by the trade depression because they lacked alternative means of livelihood. Uprooted from the land, coastal intermediaries depended on trading to obtain their food. In addition, African traders, having sought out the intermediary position during times of good trade, found themselves caught in the middle or in an uncomfortable position during the depression. European firms, also affected by the depression, charged more for imported goods, paid less for produce, and extended credit less freely. At the same time, when intermediaries attempted to pass their increased costs on to producers in the hinterland the customers complained and resisted.[180]

In addition, Sierra Leonean ascendancy was threatened by foreign competition and hostility. Lebanese traders, fleeing their poverty-stricken homeland, began showing up in Sierra Leone toward the end of the century. In the next couple of decades, they were to be the Sierra Leoneans' most serious economic competitors. European traders, as jealous of Sierra Leonean successes as the interior Africans, also threatened the Sierra Leoneans in the interior trade. The Europeans, attempting to undercut the Sierra Leonean intermediaries, began moving up the rivers in the 1870s and 1880s.[181] Individual Europeans were largely unsuccessful, but they demonstrated the vulnerability of the African intermediaries.

As the economy recovered from depression and the conditions of trade changed, European firms began to compete successfully against the Sierra Leoneans. During the depression many small traders, African and European, went bankrupt. Those Europeans with substantial financial backing in Europe survived to prosper. In the 1890s the balance of trade shifted in favor of bulk buying because now traders could use improved shipping techniques to rush large quantities to market. Large firms replaced individual traders and opened their own factories on the river. European monopolies resulted.

The hostility of the British government paralleled the growth of European competition. There had always been some hostile British officials, but toward the end of the century hostility was reinforced by a growing British racism used to justify the new stage of imperialism. Sierra Leoneans who had made successful careers as civil servants and church officials found their positions in jeopardy. The growing hostility manifested itself in attempts by the British to separate themselves physically from the Sierra Leoneans by moving to Hill Station.[182]

As intermediaries, Sierra Leoneans had profited throughout the nineteenth century from facilitating the flow of goods between the indigenous Africans, Africans outside of the hinterland area, and Europeans. Underlying tensions between the colony and interior exploded in the 1898 War, however, and these Sierra Leoneans found themselves confronted by hostility from both the Europeans and the indigenous peoples. The precipitating event was a house tax imposed by the British.

In 1895, the British declared a protectorate over the colony's hinterland. In order to finance the administration of the protectorate, expand communications, and force men into the labor market, the British imposed a tax on houses.[183] To the protectorate people the tax appeared as a symbol of the imposition of colonial rule, and they revolted. In particular, this "war for independence" was a response to: (1) the loss of authority and judicial powers by the chiefs; (2) abuses by the frontier police (the British occupying force); (3) abolition of the internal slave trade; and (4) interference by missionaries and officials in traditional customs.[184] Temne in the north coalesced around Bai Bureh, who led them in a ninemonth guerrilla campaign against the British. In turn, the British resorted to the systematic burning of villages to repress the rebellion. The Mende to the south targeted any people who appeared to represent British rule. Consequently nearly one hundred colony traders and missionaries lost their lives, and many others lost their property and fled to Freetown.[185] Their position as intrusive strangers made them particularly vulnerable.

The war occurred at a time when the kola trade was expanding in response to increased demands in The Gambia. The war's impact on the trade was decisive; kola imports declined from 12,716 hundredweight in 1897 to 10,795 in 1898, and further to 9,619 in 1899. The kola trader Priscilla A. Jones informed Sir David P. Chalmers, the special commissioner charged with the responsibility for investigating the rebellion, of her experiences in the following letter:

29th July, 1898

I trade in kola nuts, taking them in exchange for cotton, tobacco, spirits, etc. The chief of Tombay town is commonly called Beah Boy; he used to visit my husband, and my husband read a letter to the chief from the District Commissioners about the hut tax. The chief was cast down, but said he would pay the tax if he could be given three months' grace. Sammuel Cole (Jones' Boat captain) told me that my husband had been killed, and the property plundered.[186]

Many Sierra Leoneans recovered from the war; the women continued the kola trade. But as they entered the twentieth century almost totally without allies, the stage had been set for their economic decline.

Chapter 3

The Decline of Krio Women Traders
and the Crystallization of Kriodom

By the turn of the century, a new economic era had dawned in
Sierra Leone. With the introduction of banks a cash economy began displacing barter trade, and with the construction of a railway
system transportation improved and new areas were brought into
the European economic orbit. Unfortunately, Krio women entered
this new era unprepared.

Although the early 1900s signaled a new economic era that did
not include active participation by most Krio women traders, many
still continued to trade, although often on a reduced scale. Some
women traders whose businesses survived into World War I actually benefited from the war. As loyal British subjects, elite Krios in
Freetown stood firmly behind Britain in the war.[1] And like most of
British West Africa the colony and protectorate remained quiet
throughout the war.[2] Indeed, because of its natural harbor Freetown served as the headquarters of the West African Frontier
Force, the bulk of whom were from Sierra Leone, and as a fortified
naval base.[3] In addition, both the colony and the protectorate supplied Freetown-trained carriers for campaigns in Cameroon and
East Africa.[4] The sudden increase in people stationed in Freetown
had a positive economic effect on those Krio women who sold local
produce and provisions. Ruth Hollis, who was thirteen at the out-
break of the war, remembered the increased activity the war
brought to Freetown traders. She said that she helped her mother
sell vegetables on the street and that they had no problem getting
rid of their stock. "Everyone had money to spend." With the profits
made from this swift business, Hollis and her mother moved into
the Big Market in 1918 and began selling hardware and textiles.[5]

During the war Mary Williams, born in Leicester Village in 1904, began learning how to trade from her mother. Leaving at about five in the morning, every Saturday they took the long walk down the mountainside to Freetown, where Williams sold fruits while her mother sold the vegetables grown in their backyard. In 1976, Williams felt that the trade was nothing like it used to be. Now there was no longer any money in trading, but in the old days, she said, "I could feel proud of what I made from selling oranges. We lived well. Eh, no taxis then, but we didn't need them. Trading was fun."[6] Williams learned early that the quickest way to get rid of her produce was to establish "special customer" relationships. These were customers she could count on to buy from her, and Williams was particularly proud of the large number of Europeans she could count in this category.

Hollis and Williams were just two of many Krio women traders in foodstuffs for local consumption who profited by war-influenced Freetown. But for other traders, particularly those in importing and exporting, the impact of the war was more complex. Initially, Sierra Leone's exporters—like those in the rest of British West Africa—experienced an economic crisis as trade with Europe was disrupted by wartime conditions. Most important in the early stages of the war was the loss of Germany as a market. In 1913, for example, 87 percent of Sierra Leone's palm kernel products went to Germany.[7] The exporters responded to this crisis by turning from Germany to Britain as the chief market for the kernels.[8] This might have proved a satisfactory solution had not another problem arisen as the war dragged on: German submarines effectively hampered British shipping. Consequently, by 1917 the number of ships sailing into Freetown's harbor was less than half that of 1913.[9]

The slump for importers and exporters caused by the shipping shortage was short-lived because the war was soon ended. But the impact of the war on trade in Sierra Leone was more lasting, for during the war the new economic era became firmly entrenched. If it can be argued that the war was fought partly over how to divide the spoils of colonialism, then Britain had won a major battle, as she had firmly supplanted Germany as a major importer of produce not only from Sierra Leone but also from her richer and more important colonies, the Gold Coast and Nigeria.[10] Moreover, she forced German shipping out of the West African market and established a monopoly there.[11] This monopolistic arrangement further facilitated the rise of the big European firms as they established close relationships with the shipping companies.[12] Thus the First World War also helped the European firms to complete their economic war against the African intermediaries. Many African traders who had established good credit relationships with Europeans in the nineteenth century were hurt even further when the firms ceased offering favorable wholesale prices to African retailers.[13] In addition, while those Africans who imported goods such as liquor and manufactured goods found that their share of the import commerce was decreasing, those who exported produce also discovered that their portion of the export trade was diminishing.[14]

The economic depression at the end of the war, in 1920–21, demonstrated the weakness of African intermediaries throughout the region. They were unable to withstand the great fluctuations in the African produce market.[15] Taking advantage of their access to capital, the European firms, on the other hand, demonstrated their strength. Indeed, access to capital was a crucial economic advantage that the European firms held over African traders. With capital, firms could establish interior branches, hire staff on both sides of the trade, finance stocks, withstand fluctuations in trade, and ride out depressions. In addition, capital enabled firms to expand into shipping and manufacturing and thus to better influence trade. Perhaps most important, access to capital enabled European firms to buy both manufactured goods and produce in bulk and thus sell them at lower prices than their African competitors.[16]

In particular, the African elite that had emerged during the nineteenth century found itself overwhelmed by these developments. Rhoda Howard has suggested that the unequal terms of competition combined with the prohibitive cost of new technological developments forced Ghanaians out of commerce and into the professions. Despite limitations on career advancement professionals, especially those trained in law, replaced traders in the colonial administrative structure.[17] As Hopkins maintains, the elite's decline was social as well as economic and political.

Educated Christian Africans found themselves treated with less consideration after the expansion of colonial rule than they had been in the nineteenth century. Since their aspirations and life-styles were linked more closely to those of the European community than was the case with the majority of African colonial subjects, they were especially sensitive to social rebuffs stemming from racial prejudice. They were excluded from a number of commercial organizations and social clubs, some of which had begun on a multiracial basis.[18]

Moreover, the colonial elite, having supported the war effort and thus expecting representation in return, was particularly bitter over its declining influence.[19]

Among the coastal elite unable to withstand these twentieth-century developments were Sierra Leone's colony-born traders. The saga of their decline has captured much attention. Leo Spitzer has written effectively on the changing relationship between the settlers and British. In the nineteenth century, the British relied heavily on settler contributions to the colony's administration. Yet with the extension of colonial rule to the protectorate the British turned against their collaborators in what they considered to be efforts to civilize Africa. Reflecting an era of heightened racism, the British segregated themselves from the Krios and even hampered mobility within the colonial service and missionary societies.[20]

Cox-George and Allen Howard have directed attention to the economic factors in the Krios' decline. Both emphasize the economic advantages, such as access to capital, that European traders had compared to the Krios. Among other economic factors,

> the monopolistic movement among the European firms and the formation of shipping rings were the last nails to put in the coffin of the so-called African "merchant": his place being gradually taken over by the Syrian peddler-trader who now appeared on the scene.[21]

This intruding "Syrian peddler-trader" (actually from the part of Syria that is present-day Lebanon) played an important role in forcing Krios out of trade. Neil Leighton has focused on this role and the special relationship between the Lebanese and the British. West Africa was not the intended destination for the earliest

Lebanese migrants who were attempting to flee poverty and persecution in their own homeland. Bound for the New World like many other desperate migrants, they found themselves rerouted from Marseille to Dakar. From there they began to spread out along the coast, reaching Freetown by 1903.[22] West Africa's changing economic and political scene offered these new strangers opportunities that they readily grasped. They took the only role open to them during the colonial era. Unable to buy communally held land, the Lebanese could not take up commercial agriculture. Language barriers prevented them from entering the civil service. Trading provided their only means of support.[23]

The initial reaction of the British rulers was one of suspicion toward the Lebanese as they competed with Europeans to replace Krios as intermediaries. The British found Lebanese competition in the retail trade overwhelming as the latter were more willing to accept lower profit margins and bargain with African farmers. Large European firms proved too cumbersome for the task of dealing directly with the many small interior producers.[24] The need for an intermediary to ease the flow of goods across what Leighton describes as "the hiatus between the technology of the advanced sector and the subsistence sector" continued to exist.[25]

Once the British accommodated themselves to Lebanese success in this role they began to support their former competitors. Leighton makes it clear that much of Lebanese success resulted from this support.

> As a link in the chain of distribution and collection of imported goods and agricultural produce, the Lebanese received the protection of the dominant sector of colonial society—government and the larger expatriate firms.[26]

Thus indigenous Sierra Leoneans, forced to accept the Lebanese in their midst, lacked control over stranger-traders.

Moreover, the British favored the Lebanese over Krio traders. Complex reasons accounted for this British attitude. First, the British viewed the close ties between the protectorate peoples and Krios built up over the nineteenth century as a potential threat to colonial rule. If these two groups were to combine forces, Krios could lend articulate and educated voices to colonial opposition from the protectorate.[27] The Krios eventually did join the opposition because by its hold on Sierra Leone's economy, colonial rule thwarted their further economic development. As petit bourgeois traders, their aspirations were to become an independent bourgeois class dominating Sierra Leone's economy. Yet expatriate firms controlled Sierra Leone's economy and prevented development of an indigenous bourgeoisie. To ensure their own economic and political dominance, the British favored the Lebanese over the Krio comprador class.[28] As Leighton puts it:

> It would seem logical to argue that the Creoles were displaced by the Lebanese in the marketplace because of the latter's shrewdness, foreign exposure, etc. Certainly these factors played a part but the fact remains that the Europeans, because of their command of power, guaranteed the Lebanese a stake in the economic system. Although the Lebanese were good traders, adventurous, etc., the Europeans came to rely heavily on them. But the crucial variable is power—they could be controlled.[29]

Although the opposition of the British was the crucial factor in their eclipse, Krios also contributed to their own downfall. For example, they were unable to establish long-standing corporations and to adapt to the new economic conditions. But they have been overly criticized for turning away from commerce to professional occupations.[30] This view ignores both the restricted opportunities in commerce after 1898 and the power Western education gave the Krios. For example, they sat on the legislative council and thus gave it an African presence, albeit a conservative African presence.[31] They also sat on juries and prosecuted and adjudicated cases. Even today, they are overrepresented in the civil service and the professions and have an influence in Sierra Leone beyond their numerical strength of less than 2 percent of the population.[32]

Economic factors that contributed to the decline of the Krios can best be understood by focusing on the decline of Krio women traders. Colony women had used their independence well in developing a loose-knit diaspora, but in the twentieth century this independence turned into a double-edged sword. In the previous century, the small firms developed by settler women provided the kind of mobility necessary for establishing relations with African traders. As European failures demonstrated, very large firms were cumbersome. But the new era did require a scale of commercial organization larger than that of the small firms run by settler women. Although lacking the formal corporate societies based in Europe, Krios could have responded to this challenge by building family firms. Yet family ties were loose. Husbands and wives frequently went their separate ways searching for trading opportunities. Some children followed their mothers; others, their fathers.[33] As a result, large-scale corporate kinship groups rarely developed. Furthermore, women did not turn to other methods to develop larger-scale corporations. In the mid-nineteenth century when Liberated Africans first began to dominate trade, they formed small cooperative societies based on ethnic origin to increase their purchasing power.[34] But by the turn of the century much of the cohesion of these ethnic groups had broken down, and thus the Krios no longer had a basis for establishing cooperative societies. Moreover, perhaps because they had never before needed a system of clientage, they did not conceive of clients as a possible solution to forming larger-scale firms.

Their Lebanese competitors, however, found it easy to develop large-scale corporate groups. Not only did they have a strong principle of patrilineal descent, but also there were few women to compete for the sons' allegiance, especially in their early days in Sierra Leone, for Lebanese men preceded the women to Africa. When women did come, they came as wives dependent on their husbands rather than as competing traders.[35] Van der Laan has noted:

> Behind each Lebanese trader stood his wife and his sons. It was taken for granted that they would help and if necessary replace and succeed the trader. There was safety in numbers, protection against illness and death. Family ties meant that outsiders (without really understanding them) could count on the continuity of the business. A son would honor the debts of his father and would expect the repayment of credits extended by his father. The coherence of the family was the social factor which was the backbone of the success of the Lebanese traders: the authority of a man over his wife and children meant that the business was

run as resolutely as by a single person and yet was as strong as a group. It combined the strengths of individuals and of cooperation.[36]

The issue of continuity that van der Laan has raised is related to the role of inheritance. Lebanese sons could count on inheriting their fathers' property. Thus there was little confusion or dispute over what happened to a man's business after his death. But among the Krios, confusion was almost the rule after the death of a trader. Inheritance laws were based on the British legal system, and thus a person had the right to select heirs through the use of a will. By the time wills were contested and resolved, property was often so divided up among children and spouses that no one heir received enough property to have any substantial economic advantage.[37]

There were, however, signs of change in marriage practices among the Krios. At least as early as the 1880s, the most elite and literate among the Krios began advocating what they considered a Victorian marriage structure. By setting such a structure as the ideal, the elite demonstrated its distinctness, claimed as superiority, from the protectorate peoples and its closeness to the British. Complete with notions of romantic love, male elite opinion was best expressed by the *Sierra Leone Weekly News*. For example, in 1885, one writer asked:

What Men Need Wives For?

It is not to sweep the house, and make the bed, and darn the socks, and cook the meals chiefly that a man wants a wife. . . . Such things are important and the wise young man will quietly look after them. But what the true man most wants of a wife is her companionship, sympathy and love.

The way of life has many weary places in it, and man needs a companion to go with him. A man is sometimes overtaken with misfortunes; he meets with failure and defeat; trials and temptations beset him; and he needs one to stand by and sympathize. He has some stern battles to fight with poverty, with enemies, and with sin, and he needs a woman that, while he puts his arms around her and feels that he has something to fight for will help him to fight; that will put her lips to his ear and whisper words of counsel and her hand to his heart and impart new inspirations.[38]

By the turn of the century such attitudes appear to have spread to other sectors of male Krio society. This development was supported by two interrelated factors. First, as Krios lost out in commerce and turned to the professions and civil service, flexible marriage bonds that allowed men and women the freedom to roam up-country were no longer as important. Second, as Krios searched for ways to stem the tide of declining economic fortunes, less flexible bonds added to the ethnic cohesion many considered necessary.

The result, for Krio women in particular, was loss of mobility. Women who came of age in the early twentieth century complained that men attempted to force women to stay home and turn away from their trading ventures.[39] Apparently, a saying of the day was "Telling me not to trade is like telling me not to eat."[40] In their descriptions of married life in the twentieth century, some women claimed that few women worked for pay until after World War II. Office work was particularly frowned on.[41] The extension of colonial rule to the protectorate therefore brought about a decline in fortunes for all Krios, but for women this decline was particularly acute and included attempts to restrict their roles to that of housewives dominated by their husbands.

The Kola Trade

The weakness of the Krio women's economic position is demonstrated most graphically by their loss of the kola trade. Despite setbacks following the 1898 war, Sierra Leonean women entered the twentieth century firmly in control of the Sherbro-based kola trade. Although the disturbances caused exports to fall in 1898 and 1899, the women renewed their trading efforts. Consequently, by 1900 exports reached a new high in both quantity and value.

Success brought attention; competition followed. While the British may have scorned this intra-African trade in earlier days, the wealth that accrued from the trade eventually attracted them. Moreover, as European traders were beginning to move up the rivers they came into closer contact with the ultimate producers and consumers of trade goods. Thus about 1906 the Europeans

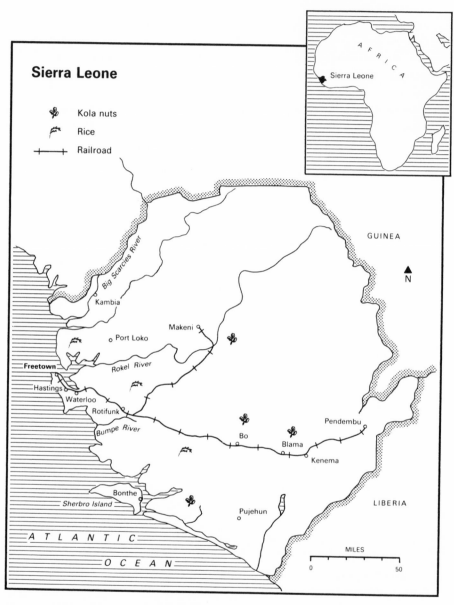

Map 2. Sources of Kola and Rice Trade around 1920. (Adapted from John I. Clarke, ed., *Sierra Leone in Maps* [London, 1966], pp. 75, 105.)

entered the kola nut trade.[42] Following a pattern typical of most European interior trade, the Europeans did not venture far from their river factories in search of the kola nuts; instead, they waited for the kola to be brought to them. The Sierra Leoneans, who already had the necessary contacts, supplied kola to European firms, which subsequently shipped it to their branches in Dakar, Bathurst, and Bissau.[43] Because of their high overhead, the Europeans did not threaten the Sierra Leonean women's domination of the trade. While the European firms were barely making profits, the Sierra Leoneans were reportedly claiming profits of 214 to 316 percent.[44]

What the European firms could not do, the Lebanese did with ease. The colonial government first recognized Lebanese participation in the kola trade in 1913. Two years later, the Lebanese dominated the trade.[45] Unlike the European firms, the Lebanese traders went directly to the source of the kola nuts, and taking advantage of the extension of the railway they opened up new areas such as Blama and Bo to kola collection.[46]

Krio women continued to export kola, but their percentage of the trade declined drastically even as imports increased. In the nineteenth century the kola trade had been principally a labor-intensive trade that Krio women found easy to control. But demand in the savanna regions continued to rise, and a new requirement, capital, was needed to remain competitive. The European firms lacked the labor; the Krio women, the capital. The Lebanese combined their own labor with capital and captured the kola trade.

Krio women were stunned. How, in two short years, could they lose control of a profitable and long-standing trade staple to the Lebanese? Lucy Tucker of Bonthe, who helped her mother in the kola trade, said that the harder Krio women tried, the easier it seemed for the Lebanese. As she and her mother traveled up the rivers they searched out more producers than ever before. Yet although they continued to trade in kola nuts into the 1940s, by about 1920 they had started selling most of their nuts to Lebanese intermediaries instead of shipping them directly to Bathurst and Bissau as they had done previously.[47]

Although Judy Vincent, in 1977 the oldest living former Big Market trader, never participated in the kola trade herself, she watched the decline of Krio women's participation in the trade

from the Big Market. Women, she claimed, continued to trade in
kola nuts and even to export them to Senegambia, but all they
could speak about was the intrusion of the Lebanese into the kola
market. The change was so spectacular that some wondered what
magic the Lebanese used.[48]

Unfortunately for the Krio women, the Lebanese secured the
dominant position in the new areas of kola supply where the
women had yet to build long-standing commercial relations. In the
older supply areas, principally along the coastal belt which could be
reached by waterborne transportation, women continued to dominate.[49] But the Lebanese control of the new supply areas gave
them a competitive edge. Soon kola from Lebanese-controlled rail-
borne supplies exceeded kola from the coastal belt. Moreover, a
change in the Senegambian region affected the relative positions of
the Lebanese and Krio women in the trade. Up until 1904, The
Gambia received the largest share of the kola exported to Senegambia. But as Dakar began to emerge as the major port in the
region, the largest bulk of the exports began flowing there. The
Krio's network was better established in The Gambia than in Senegal. The Lebanese firmly established themselves in Dakar and thus
were in a better position to take advantage of the growing importance of its port.[50]

The Lebanese had similar successes in capturing control of
other commodities. Principal among these was rice. Although
Krios, both male and female, were the first to send rice to Freetown
by rail, the Lebanese who entered the rice trade in 1910 soon
wrenched control of the Freetown rice market from the people
who had dominated it for almost a century. While the Krios continued to dominate the waterborne rice trade, the Lebanese controlled the rail-borne trade, thereby capturing the largest share of
the Freetown market.[51]

The Lebanese domination of the rice and kola markets contributed to the animosities in Sierra Leone that eventually led to anti-
Lebanese riots in July, 1919. In part, the riots resulted from the
dislocations caused by the war. As part of the war effort, more
people moved into Freetown than the local distribution system
could feed. For those traders involved in selling produce for local
consumption, the increased immigration was a bonanza, for they
had little trouble selling out their stocks. But such a situation indicates a food deficit. Indeed, severe food shortages did occur.[52]

Freetownians began to accuse the Lebanese of hoarding rice to drive up the price; and this accusation was partly substantiated in June, 1919, when three Lebanese traders were prosecuted and found guilty of charging more than the allotted price for rice.[53]

Coincident with the growing hostilities and food shortages was a strike by railway workers who felt they had been cheated out of a war bonus that other government workers had received. The strike, although prompted by a minor issue, erupted into "anti-Syrian" riots. One week later the riots spread up-country, although they never reached the fervor of the Freetown riots. But even in Freetown, only three "Syrians" lost their lives: one accidentally shot by a fellow Syrian, one in premature childbirth brought on by the riot, and one from a beating received from the rioters. The major target of the rioters was property. Both in Freetown and up-country several Lebanese shops were looted. The First West India Regiment and police restored order after making 245 arrests.[54]

The government, which had failed miserably to respond to the food shortage in Freetown, placed all the blame for the riots on the Krios.[55] In accusing the Krios of organizing the riots, the government may have felt its fears of a potential protectorate-Krio coalition were near realization. The Krios clearly had grievances, many of which were vented during the riots. While many non-Krios joined the riots, there is no evidence of an organized attack on the Lebanese. Following the riots the Krios expressed their grievances against the Lebanese traders directly to the government and in the press. The Krios complained to the governor that besides cheating and hoarding foodstuffs during times of severe shortages, the Lebanese had unfairly taken over the trade of the Krio women traders.[56] Yet the Krios claimed that they were not jealous of the Lebanese, as others had alleged:

> Trade Jealousy! and our tradeswomen have been calling Syrians, 'master, master' and have calmly let them rule the Kola Nut Trade. Does any white man think that if it came to a matter of real competition where Sierra Leoneans are determined, the Syrians could beat them in their own field?[57]

There is no doubt that the loss of the kola trade by the Krio women infuriated all Krios. Writing in 1919 for the Krio-controlled *Sierra Leone Weekly News*, "Emile," in an article entitled "The Syrian Peril," urged all good Sierra Leoneans not to do business with the Lebanese kola traders.[58]

The threat of the Lebanese traders extended beyond Sierra Leone's borders, and as the following article, "The Ugly Syrian Domination in West Africa," demonstrates, resentment had not lessened by June, 1920.

> But the local Syrian is murdering us, and enjoys it. Let traders tell their tales of woe in the matter of Kola Nuts trading from here to the Gambia, Senegal, and the blood of the listener will curdle. . . . All along the banks of the Gambia these Syrians are at the throats of the Chiefs with their Kola baskets. In our Protectorate it is the same. Can't we do the same? We can do it. . . . O Creoles! Your well being is in your hands. Don't you know that those who will be free *themselves* must strike the first blow? And did not the old Roman speak the truth who declared that those who want peace should prepare for war? Creoles of West Africa! What is the matter?[59]

The war never materialized; the riots were like the last kicks of a dying horse. As the War of 1898 and its aftermath symbolized the break between the Krios and the British government, so the anti-Syrian riots and their aftermath signified the cementing of relations between the Lebanese and the British. As a demonstration of their support of the Lebanese, the government assessed the Freetown ratepayers £36,635 as compensation to the Lebanese who lost their property. The Krios balked at this stiff fine and complained that up-country people who had rioted were not required to help compensate the Lebanese and that Krios had not been given similar compensation in 1898. Backing down from this original demand, the government instead required the Freetown City Council to pay the government five hundred pounds a year for ten years. [60] Thus the riots also demonstrated that the rift between the Krios and the British was irreparable.

Despite such major setbacks, Krios continued to trade. And despite growing hostility from Krio men, many women still pursued the produce trade; their share of the market was greatly reduced, however, and often they sold their goods to Lebanese traders who either retained the produce or sold it in bulk to European firms.[61]

Sarian During from Leicester Village said she continued to leave that mountain village with her garden vegetables for Freetown at 6:00 A.M. every Tuesday, Thursday, and Saturday. Her mother had traded in the same fashion, but unlike her mother who sold to Europeans, During found the Lebanese were her best customers. Even when she was lucky to sell all her produce to the same trader, however, the most profit she could make in a day was four pounds.[62] Women also began buying imported goods from Lebanese traders instead of directly from the European firms.[63]

The Big Market Declines

The fortunes of the Big Market, the Krio women's central market, paralleled the fortunes of these traders. Many of the market's traders survived into the twentieth century; those who did not were quickly replaced. Despite economic hardships, by World War I the marketplace had become even busier than ever. During the war, in fact, the services of the central market were in greater demand than ever before, as the traders helped supply the many British soldiers who passed through Freetown. Since Freetown was the headquarters of the West African Frontier Force and a fortified naval base, the number of British soldiers stationed there was considerable.[64]

Big Market vendors were particularly glad to see Australian troops land at Freetown because the latter had gained a reputation as big spenders.[65] A British officer who arrived in Freetown toward the end of the war with twenty thousand Australian troops was fascinated by what he saw at the Big Market:

Entering the market . . . one soon became interested in and surrounded by the sellers, of both sexes and every age. Frequently inquiries were made as to whether the [twenty thousand Australian] troops were going to land, the reason being, as one trader told me, "Australians have plenty money." They certainly spent a good deal in Freetown. The market was stocked with the usual wares, and fruit of all kinds was abundant, and to our ideas cheap, and the sellers proved fully competent at driving a bargain! One feature I noticed, as showing business acumen, was the next day, when the troops landed, many things in the market had increased 50 percent, in some cases 100 percent; but despite this fact, in a few hours the market was sold out, fruit vendors and the sellers of picture postcards in particular doing a thriving trade.[66]

Unfortunately, the prosperity that accrued from World War I only masked the realities of a new economic order that did not include a central role for the Big Market. The colonial government, which had relied heavily on the Big Market during the war, increasingly turned to British firms, such as Cold Storage Ltd., for provisions. The firms themselves, moreoever, increasingly used Lebanese intermediaries instead of the Big Market traders. Within the economic hierarchy, the Big Market became just one of the markets through which produce flowed. Similarly, imported items were no longer as likely to pass directly from the European firms to the Big Market. Now the traders found that they had to purchase their goods from Lebanese intermediaries as the European merchants became increasingly distant and inaccessible.

The decline of Krio women traders is reflected in the Big Market's decline. First, like other Krio women, most Big Market traders lacked the capital to maintain a prominent role in the twentieth-century economy. Second, they found that their contacts for local produce were concentrated along the coastal belt in an era when rail-borne trade from the interior began to dominate the Freetown market. Since Krio women in general were unable to establish themselves in this new interior trade, Big Market traders did not have the necessary contacts for building up new trading networks.

Judy Victoria Vincent, alias Mami Abiose, witnessed many of the Big Market's changes. Born around 1880 to a Big Market trader, Mami Abiose spent her early childhood around the marketplace where she helped her mother, Judy Pratt, and grandmother, Sarah Pratt, sell cotton goods and vegetables. Mami Abiose's grandmother Sarah began selling vegetables under a tree near Government Wharf in the 1850s and accumulated enough capital to join the Big Market traders during the first year it opened. Mami Abiose described her as a foundation seller at the Big Market. Sarah Pratt was soon joined by her daughter Judy. While the Pratts never ventured into importing items on a large scale, they occasionally gave money to Big Market trader Mami Kude, who would go to

England to buy cotton goods from the Krio merchant Malama Thomas, as well as from the European firm of Patterson, Zochonis, Ltd. (PZ). British cloth was not the only cotton goods the Pratts sold, however. In addition they imported cloth from Lagos, where they had family connections, and from Conakry.[67]

The Pratts established regular vegetable suppliers from Bullom shore for rice and green leaves and suppliers from the mountain villages for garden vegetables; the suppliers received credit for cloth purchased from the Pratts.

By World War I Mami Abiose had taken over the Pratt stall. She remembered those prosperous days well. The Big Market, she claimed, had never been so busy—the traders could barely keep up with the demand. She remembered the landing of the Australian troops; they purchased goods with gold and silver, she claimed.[68] But almost as abruptly as prosperity came, it ended. While she continued to deal with Malama Thomas for cotton goods, PZ refused to extend credit to her. She had felt comfortable with her "special customer" relationship with PZ, for it extended back two generations. Now she was forced to establish a wholesaler-retailer bond with Lebanese traders. And she even lost some of her regular produce suppliers to Lebanese traders.

In 1919, when hostilities broke out against Lebanese traders, Mami Abiose did not join the rioters, but she claimed that she and many of the other Big Market traders identified with the anger expressed by the riots. It seemed to the traders that the Lebanese had risen from nowhere to usurp their comfortable intermediary role.

Although the Big Market traders did not riot in 1919, they later expressed their anxiety about their precarious economic position by joining the protest movements of the late 1930s and 1940s. Many of the most prominent members of the Sierra Leone Market-women's Union traded at the Big Market. One such woman was Mary Martyn, who as an officer of the union signed a petition asking for the release from detention of I. T. A. Wallace-Johnson, the Krio trade unionist and journalist.[69] Martyn had traded at the Big Market during its heyday. From her profits she was able to pay her own way to England and take her nephew with her. Perhaps the experience of watching the once-thriving market deteriorate influenced her decision to become politically involved.

No longer a central market, the Big Market developed specialties for which it is famous today. Most prominent and visible of these specialties are dry goods items (i.e., locally manufactured spoons, baskets, and mats), recycled imported goods (i.e., cans, bottles, and nails), and Sierra Leonean art (i.e., Bundu masks, carved animals, and beads). Less visible, but perhaps most important, is the trade in local medicine. It is said that one can get any kind of indigenous medicine in this market; and it is for the sale of these medicines that the Big Market vendors are best known today. (Some believe that the traders never bother to lock the market because no one would dare offend the traders by stealing their goods. This belief persists despite the two huge padlocks found at each end of the market.)

The women sell medicines that come from as far away as Nigeria. Indeed, it is partly because of their Nigerian heritage that Big Market women are supposed to have intimate knowledge of powerful medicines, for the Sierra Leoneans believe that the Yoruba are especially skilled with herbs.[70] Krio women have combined the medical knowledge learned in Bundu with what they learned from their mothers and in the Hunting Societies. With that knowledge they have turned the Big Market into the largest pharmacy in Sierra Leone.

While the Big Market no longer presents a picture of successful commercial activity, the present and former vendors remain proud of its traditions. They are especially proud of the children of Big Market traders, as it is widely believed that the sons and daughters of Big Market traders have done especially well since the old traders could afford to give them good educations. When Teddy Jones and Mami Abiose got together, their conversation often turned to this subject. Mami Pray, who led the Big Market traders in prayer twice a day, was the mother of a well-respected minister, Rev. M. J. C. Cole.[71] Mami Decker sent her son to law school in London and Mami Lucas's grandson became a judge.[72] But most prominent of the Big Market offspring were Abi Jones's children, who included an Anglican bishop and a prominent doctor.[73]

These successful children represent past glories. By World War II the days when the Big Market functioned as a central market and assisted in the flow of goods up and down the economic hierarchy had passed. Similarly, the market no longer served as a center for Krio cultural integration and diffusion. By the 1950s, when the main wharf was moved from Government Wharf to Cline Town at the eastern end of Freetown, the Big Market had already declined to a minor market where fruits and vegetables were no longer sold and little boys teased old traders about their peculiar trade in herbs and medicines.[74] Long before the harbor was built at Cline Town, the center of the transportation network had moved away from the wharf, where the coastal trade had been focused, to the railroad depot, and the Big Market stood isolated from the center of commercial activity.

The Diaspora Contracts

Krio women trading outside the peninsula also experienced changes. In Bonthe, where Krio women had once controlled part of its thriving trade, the whole town experienced an economic decline. First, Freetown, because of its deep harbor, captured much of Bonthe's overseas trade. But because of their position at the mouth of an extensive riverine trading network Bonthe traders continued to take an active part in Freetown's trade, occasionally shipping goods abroad although more often shipping produce to Freetown. The coming of the railroad had serious consequences for Bonthe, however, as rail-borne trade began to outstrip the waterborne trade. New markets were opened in the interior, and those Krio women traders who were based in Bonthe and elsewhere along the coast found themselves at an economic disadvantage.[75]

Although women continued to travel up the rivers searching for rice and kola nuts, they increasingly sold their produce to Lebanese traders based in Bonthe and Freetown.[76] By the 1920s the scale of Krio women's trade in Bonthe was noticeably smaller. Markets on Victoria Road and Heddle Road near the wharf, which had once thrived, now lost most of their vitality.[77] Whereas earlier women traders built homes in Bonthe as an investment for their profits, fewer Krio women had this option after the 1920s. Those who had been fortunate enough to build houses before the economic decline of Bonthe continued to make some money from rent. But unlike Freetown, where property remained valuable, Bonthe property depreciated because the town itself was in economic eclipse.[78]

Thus over the years Bonthe has declined to the point where today an unsuspecting observer would not guess that this quiet town was once a center of brisk trade.[79]

Women who recognized early that the trade along the coastal belt was deteriorating left for the new railway towns. In 1918, when George Smith of Leicester Village was twenty-one, he moved to Blama to be with his mother, Edna Wright. She had decided in 1916 to transfer her business from Bonthe to take advantage of the railway that ran through Blama. Once in Blama, she opened a shop selling headties, cloth, and tobacco. Although she managed to stay in business until 1940, when she returned to Leicester, the profits she anticipated never materialized and her trade remained on a small scale.[80] Other Krio women who attempted to take advantage of this railway town included Joanna Smith and Stella Parker, both of whom also owned shops and, like Edna Wright, purchased goods from both Lebanese traders and European firms.[81] Other railway towns also attracted similar small-scale women traders. Mary Beckles of Kent claimed that a number of women from her village regularly took the train to Rotifunk and Moyamba to trade.[82]

Although trading remained the preferred occupation for most Krio women, many found that they had to turn elsewhere to supplement their declining incomes. Since they had been trained as seamstresses in school, many women took up sewing as an alternative to full-time trading. Bure Palmer, whose biography is detailed in chapter 4, was one such woman.

The general trend for Krio women traders was clearly one of economic decline. Many women maintained their businesses, however, and some women prospered. Princess James's life exemplifies this latter case. James's maternal grandfather, Ayo Beckley, an Afro-American who emigrated to Sierra Leone when he was a small boy, was sent back to the United States to learn the construction trade. He eventually shared his knowledge with his son-in-law, James's father Peter Grisborne Thomas. Together they built several prominent buildings around Freetown, including Wesley Methodist and Dove Memorial churches.[83] Peter Thomas, a descendant of Igbo Recaptives, combined his construction trade with trade in fruit and garden vegetables. He and James's mother shipped kola nuts to The Gambia. Together Princess James's parents built a successful business, a fact that influenced her life. "Every week I watched my father and mother counting hundreds of pounds and I got quite used to seeing money around."[84]

In addition to the early training James had in business, she also went to school to learn nursing. But while she only earned fifteen pounds a month as a nurse, she built up a trade on the side that brought in about forty to fifty pounds per week, for with capital from her parents she had begun importing hats and dresses through British catalogues for a total value of up to three hundred pounds.[85]

James continued this trade until 1943, when she married and her husband objected to her trading. She was, however, much too strong willed to be prevented from trading for very long. As a nurse at Hill Station Hospital, where the British and other Europeans went, James built up crucial relationships, which she exploited once she began trading again.[86]

James's real successes came after the period under study in this book, but they demonstrate the skills that she had learned in the earlier period. Princess James stayed at Hill Station for only a year; in 1944 she opened a shop, on Freetown's Pademba Road, worth eight thousand pounds. And in 1946 she opened an additional shop.[87] To stock these shops she used the contacts made at Hill Station and received favorable wholesale deals from the companies. The manager of United Africa Company (UAC) was particularly helpful because he gave her advance notice of closed clearance sales. "I would be the only Sierra Leone woman at these sales; the place was filled with Lebanese traders. I got this privilege because I was different; UAC, PZ, all of them knew they could count on me."[88]

Nonetheless, James felt that opportunities in Freetown were limited, and so in 1947 she moved to Koindu near the Guinean and Liberian borders.[89] She had identified Koindu as a fertile area for trade when passing through to Guinea searching for a cure for her sick sister. Feeling that Guinea lacked many imported goods, she made contacts with business people there. At the time, Koindu was a small market. After she arrived, she hired an interpreter who traveled to Liberia and Guinea advertising her store. Traveling to Freetown weekly, she stocked her store well, and since UAC backed her with credit, she offered a variety of goods. "That's why I like the Englishmen, if you're pushful they help you."[90]

James helped develop the international market that continues to flourish in Koindu today.[91] But success did not come easily. Soon after opening, her shop was burglarized and she lost goods worth three hundred pounds. In 1948, when she was trying to make her building burglarproof, a fire started that killed many of the town's animals, and to avoid prosecution she had to bribe the town clerk to keep her case out of court. Fire struck again in 1956. When a small boy attempting to steal gasoline from one of her lorries lit a match, five and a half barrels of petrol blew up, destroying part of her shop.[92]

Yet her major problem came when her success attracted Lebanese traders. "When I got to Koindu there were very few Lebanese traders there. They only had a few small shops and were not even allowed to stay there. They bought a little produce, not much else." But in the 1950s the Lebanese began moving into Koindu in large numbers. According to James, they attempted to drive her out of business. She held her own until the 1960s, when she decided it was time to move on to diamond mining. While she continues to hold property in Koindu, she rented her shop to Lebanese traders until it burned down in 1979.[93]

From her business in Koindu, James had more capital than she needed to purchase a license from the government and begin mining. Mining for diamonds found just below the surface did not require much capital. Additional expenses included only the cost of shovels and the salary of the diggers who actually prospected her diamond fields. Her success in diamond mining after moving to Kono in 1964 far exceeded any earlier successes. In the light of van der Laan's contention that Krios—unlike the Temne, Mende, and Kono—rarely entered diamond mining, her success appears particularly outstanding.[94] Like other successful Africans in the trade, she has demonstrated considerable technical, organizational, and commercial skills. One of her sons manages an office that she has opened in Germany. In 1976 she had enough resources to divert a river off her mining concession. And her daughter, Tunde James, was exploring business opportunities in Nigeria with an aunt who had recently retired from the Nigerian civil service. By 1983 the daughter had switched her attention largely to the United States, where she made frequent business trips.[95] In the late 1970s James and her family expanded into the transportation industry. This new company, James International, grew into one of the two largest transportation companies in Sierra Leone.[96]

Wealth has brought political power. In 1976 the minister of the interior, whose responsibilities included the diamond area, and his wife attended her sixtieth birthday party. One of their daughters was being raised by James, an arrangement cementing their political relationship. In addition, several political leaders and businessmen from the diamond region stay at her commodious house when they go to Freetown.

Princess James's life represents the realization of a dream that many other Krio women had but few were able to fulfill. She combined political and commercial power in a manner reminiscent of such early settlers as Mary Perth and Betsy Carew. Unfortunately, since the turn of the century few Krio women have obtained this kind of commercial strength. In response to their declining power, they searched with their men for political solutions.

The Evolution of Kriodom

Increasingly Krios viewed themselves as a cohesive ethnic group. Divisions between Aku, Igbo, Nova Scotians, and Maroons, while remembered, lost importance as Krios banded together to confront their declining political and economic fortunes. Their isolated position within Sierra Leone even led them to look for outside allies. For example, Krios played prominent roles in the National Congress of British West Africa, an organization founded in 1920 to represent the English-speaking coastal elite's interests. They also established a branch of Marcus Garvey's United Negro Improvement Association.[97]

The developing ethnic cohesion among the Krios reflected a change in the nature of ethnic boundaries within Sierra Leone. In the nineteenth century ethnicity became an increasingly important factor in the political and economic scene as people competed for jobs, formed trading groups, and established political alliances.[98] But the early twentieth century witnessed a significant increase in ethnic rivalry as the expansion of colonial rule forced people to identify themselves first by their ethnic identity. Indeed, British policy heightened rivalry between ethnic groups to ensure hostility between the various ethnic groups and thwart the development of a panethnic anticolonial movement. J. B. Webster maintains that this colonial policy was demonstrated by the establishment of the Bo School for the sons of Mende chiefs.

"Bo School was specifically designed to strengthen Mende ethnic consciousness. . . . The students of Bo were to be so fashioned that they would never feel sympathy with or be tempted into a partnership with the Creoles of Freetown."[99]

The tendency toward a Mende-Temne alliance was threatened by the greater educational opportunities that the British offered the Mende.[100]

In contrast, the relatively flexible ethnic boundaries of the nineteenth century encouraged women who sought economic gain and personal independence to become Sierra Leonean traders, even if they were originally Mende or Temne. In the twentieth century, when the definition of Sierra Leonean changed to include all Africans living within the colony and protectorate, a new identity had to be established for women from the colony who acted as stranger-traders. This new identity, Krio, lumped all colony-born strangers together and included negative images fostered by declining economic fortunes and propaganda from the colonial rulers.

The Krios' changing occupational base from commerce to salaried positions further exacerbated this situation. As traders in the interior, the colony-born women maintained close ties with the interior peoples. But as women became civil servants and professionals based mainly in Freetown, the need for close contact declined. A woman who turned from trading up-country to teaching Krio children in a Freetown school had less need to communicate with Mende or Sherbro women; a major restraint on barriers between Krios and others had been removed. Moreover, the changes in marriage patterns accompanying the changes in occupational base reflected the differentiation between Krios and other Africans. Marriage partners were more clearly defined as including all settler groups but excluding others. Increased attention to marriage partners coincided with tighter family control over female sexuality. Not only did the mobility that allowed women to trade and control their own sexuality decrease, but also their pool of possible marriage partners contracted. This change cannot be explained simply as a result of male desires to control women; for many women benefited as well. All Krios had a stake in tighter ethnic cohesion and thus older women also acted to restrict younger women's marriage options.

Although boundary crystallization was the general trend in post-1898 Sierra Leone, there were tendencies in the other direction. Founded in 1938, the West African Youth League articulated the desire of some Krios to maintain close relations with other Sierra Leoneans. The youth league, part of a larger movement in British West Africa, was a response to the vacuum created by the demise of the National Congress of British West Africa.[101] Led by younger and more militant leaders, such youth organizations were more activist than the National Congress. In Sierra Leone, the youth league was founded by I. T. A. Wallace-Johnson, "a trade unionizer, militant journalist, nationalist political leader and Pan-Africanist."[102] Besides attempting to unite all Sierra Leoneans, the league offered a more active role to women. Most prominent among the female members of the youth league was Constance Cummings-John. When the youth league captured all the seats in Freetown's municipal council elections in December, 1938, she and her colleague, Mr. E. A. C. Davies, polled more than three times the votes of any other candidates in the central ward. She became the first woman to occupy such an office in West Africa.[103]

Cummings-John had returned home earlier that year from London, where she had been introduced to Pan-African ideas. But it was her experiences as a student in the United States during the early 1930s that made her receptive to these ideas. She claimed that her first-hand knowledge of racism in the United States had politicized her, much as Kwame Nkrumah had been radicalized during his student days in the United States.[104] Shortly after returning to Sierra Leone, Cummings-John began to organize by forming a branch of the London-based League of Colored Peoples.[105] When Wallace-Johnson reached Freetown later that year, they became close political allies.

In 1939, as part of an effort to insure that Sierra Leoneans remained quiescent during World War II, the colonial government arrested Wallace-Johnson.[106] Cummings-John took an active role in agitating for his freedom, bringing with her the support of other Krio women through the Sierra Leone Marketwomen's Union which she had founded.[107] The colonial government utilized extraordinary powers granted during wartime to keep Wallace-Johnson interned and thus isolated from his followers. Cummings-John's political career, however, was just getting started. During the political drama leading to independence, she supported the Sierra Leone People's Party, bringing with her the support of the Sierra Leone Women's Association, which she had founded in 1951.[108] Her greatest triumph came in 1964 when she was appointed mayor of Freetown.[109]

Cummings-John's life was exceptional. For most Krio women, the twentieth century has been characterized by economic decline and political frustration. Replaced by the Lebanese as economic intermediaries and by the protectorate women as retailers, Krio women have had to turn away from trade to the professions. In doing so, they joined with Krio men in the crystallization of Kriodom.

Chapter 4

The Spirit of Krio Women Traders:
Three Biographical Sketches

The biographies presented here evoke the spirit of the settler women traders and bring to life their concerns and struggles. The women, Bure Charlotte Palmer, Lillie Mae Domingo, and Abigail Jones, will not be found in the annals of elite political history, but their lives are important. Too often people who are not from the elite classes are viewed as a statistical mass, devoid of individual personalities. In such a view, "the masses" respond monolithically, while dominating and lively individuals direct the trends of history. Imperfect as they may be because of the interviewers' and interpreters' biases, oral histories can penetrate beneath the surface of the statistics and open our view to the complexities of social, political, and economic forces.

Palmer, Domingo, and Jones each had individual and private concerns; nonetheless their individual lives, both when viewed separately and when taken as a whole, highlight issues in the lives of many settler women traders. Like many other Krio women, they valued education, embraced Christianity, and manipulated their economic environment. With other Krio women, they struggled to stem the tide of a declining diaspora. Their differences serve to highlight the complexities of Krio life in the twentieth century. Even Jones's success as a businesswoman underscores the obstacles confronting all Krio women, for it demonstrates the possible solutions others could not find.[1]

All of these women faced an era of economic decline for Krio traders. The extension of the colony to include all of present-day Sierra Leone changed the terms under which they attempted to trade. Two of the three women lost family members in the protectorate peoples' 1898 struggle against taxes—the first major intrusion of the colonial state. All of them faced fierce competition from Lebanese traders who moved into the lucrative kola and rice trades that settler women once dominated. Unable to tap into European networks, these traders were at a disadvantage compared to the more favored Lebanese. Despite the parameters set by changes in the world economy and the hostility of the colonial state, these women adapted to the challenges and changes of the twentieth century.

The Making of a Krio Woman Trader:
Bure Charlotte Palmer

Trading in late nineteenth- and early twentieth-century Sierra Leone was a highly competitive business fraught with financial risks. Settler women began their training for this occupation as little girls, serving apprenticeships with their mothers and/or other female relatives. Bure Charlotte Palmer's life story illustrates the kind of preparation women went through to become traders. Her biography demonstrates how she developed and used her skills and how these skills proved inadequate in the face of Lebanese competition. Born in 1892 of Igbo and Yoruba descent, Bure Palmer remembered events that occurred even before the 1898 war. As a little girl, she would visit her aunt, Nancy Kenny, up-country. Traveling between Kalihun, Bonthe, and York Island, Palmer accompanied Kenny on her business and evangelical trips. Kenny viewed her "labors" as inseparably intertwined. She would not have considered trading without attempting to spread Christianity. During her visits with her aunt, Palmer learned to speak Mende and Temne, two languages she used later in her own trading ventures.[2]

Palmer's appenticeship with Kenny ended abruptly and dramatically when her aunt was murdered in the 1898 war.[3] Not surprisingly, the missionary-trader Kenny was a prime target for hostility in the protectorate because she was a visible symbol of the hated alien British rule. Fortunately, Palmer was in Freetown at the time of the war. Tragically, she lost not only her aunt but also her father, W. T. George, a Methodist preacher at Bonthe. Years later Palmer looked back on that time with pride as she noted that her aunt and father had died "in the service of the Lord."

Although Palmer continued to visit other female relatives trading up-country, her most intimate and formative experience with trading came at the center of Krio women's trade, the Big Market. Palmer learned the crucial details of trading from her mother, Ruth George, a produce vendor, and she also observed the operations of Big Market traders like Abi Jones. Palmer was fortunate to be an apprentice in this bustling economic center during its most prosperous years. There she watched trade conducted on several levels: traders buying produce from the mountain villages and Bullom shore and then selling the produce to European firms; women negotiating with European firms to purchase imported goods in order to sell these goods to local retailers; and women "bulking" produce for sale to government institutions such as hospitals and military units. During World War I Palmer observed and participated in the frantic activity of keeping the British forces supplied.[4]

As important as the hours that Palmer spent at the Big Market were, she had to share her time with an equally important aspect of her education, her formal schooling. With profits from her produce trade Ruth George paid her daughter's school fees through her graduation from Buxton Memorial School and Female Educational Institute, where she concentrated on dressmaking.[5] Ruth George wanted her to learn trading, but she also stressed the need for Palmer to be prepared for life outside the business world. In the first decade of the twentieth century, business thrived. Nonetheless, the risks of financial failure were high and George remembered the depressed economy of the 1880s. Consequently she wanted Palmer to have a profession as a backup in the event their business failed.

By 1915, when Bure Palmer married Matru Palmer, a controller of customs with whom she eventually had three children, she was a well-educated and well-rounded young woman ready for the life of a trader and teacher. When Matru Palmer was promoted to a post in Bathurst, The Gambia, in 1917, he took his young wife with him.[6] Despite the emotional strain that separation from her family could have caused, moving to Bathurst with her husband was opportune for Palmer because it enabled her to expand her business with her mother. Earlier they had begun trading in kola nuts on a small scale although they had always sold them to intermediaries for export. With Palmer's move to the savanna region, intermediaries were no longer needed. Now Ruth George shipped the kola to Palmer, who made good profits by selling them wholesale directly to Gambian women retailers. With the profits from the kola nut sales, Palmer could buy peanuts and ship them to Freetown, where her mother sold them at the Big Market.[7]

In developing this lucrative arrangement Palmer and her mother repeated the pattern of many Krio women. Few women missed the opportunity to establish trading networks when their husbands were transferred to jobs in other colonies by the government or European firms. If a wife found herself in the savanna region, she most likely traded in kola nuts and peanuts. But other items were traded, too. For example, cloth dyed or manufactured in Sierra Leone could be sold in The Gambia, while Gambian cloth could be shipped to Freetown for sale. Similarly, Palmer sent her mother Gambian cloth to sell. Through such networks, Krio women established important intra–West African economic links.

An energetic young woman, Palmer worked at a number of projects besides her import/export business. Six days a week she rose at 3:00 A.M. to bake bread to be sold during the day. Using her house as a shop, she also sold goods ordered from German and American catalogues, print cloth used for Krio-style dresses, and Madras cloth used for headties. In addition, in the afternoons she would train young girls in dressmaking. Profits that were the result of her enormous effort and shrewdness enabled her to spend one vacation in London during 1921. On two other occasions, she planned to visit London but both times became ill en route and was unable to continue beyond the Canary Islands. Making a trip to the metropolis was, of course, symbolic of elite status for many of the colonists, and Palmer spoke of her trip as a demonstration of the high status she held in Krio society, a society that extended throughout West Africa.[8]

For the eighteen years Palmer lived in The Gambia, she carried on her import/export trade, sold bread, and trained other young girls to become dressmakers. This phase of her life ended abruptly in 1935 when her husband died and she returned to Freetown to be with her family. Having become an integral part of the Bathurst commercial community, Palmer remembered her years there fondly. Prominent among these memories was her connection with the church. To Palmer, her achievements as a trader were insignificant compared to her life as a Christian. She was particularly proud of the number of church organizations to which she belonged in both Bathurst and Freetown, and she wished to be certain that anything written about her would emphasize her dedication to the church and Christian principles.

The experiences and attitudes that bound them to the church aided Krios when they left Sierra Leone because they provided them with a sense of belonging to the wider Christian community. Thus in Bathurst, Palmer was able to feel comfortable when she joined a community of Christians she had never known before. Membership in the Christian church gave Palmer much of the emotional support she needed when she was far away from home. In addition, it aided her business. At church meetings Palmer met other Sierra Leoneans residing in The Gambia, as well as Christianized Gambian women. Some of these women sent their daughters to learn dressmaking from their fellow Christian Bure Palmer. And from these women came Palmer's best trading contacts.[9] Thus Christianity helped establish a valuable identity that served to bind expatriate Krios to one another and to other Christianized Africans. By locating the appropriate church in Bathurst, Accra, or Calabar, an uprooted Krio could identify not only people who shared similar religious views but also those with common economic interests.[10]

Upon her return to Freetown after her husband's death, Palmer attempted to continue her import/export business, using contacts she had made in Bathurst. But her years in The Gambia represented the pinnacle of her business career. Increasingly, Palmer and her mother found it difficult to ship kola directly to their Gambian agents; it was easier to sell them to Lebanese intermediaries who could assure their sale in the Senegambian region. This change caused the profits from her trade to decline rapidly. Palmer's inability to sustain reliable contacts in The Gambia and to maintain her business in Freetown underscores the collapse of the Krio women's trading diaspora. By the 1930s, the cohesion of the commercial diaspora had long since dissipated, and most networks were in disarray. Palmer did not discuss the specific reasons for the failure of her import/export business; nonetheless, it is possible that after the collapse of the diaspora she could find no suitable and trustworthy agents. While she was in Bathurst, she ran a one-woman business and never established a firm that could withstand her absence.[11] Once she returned to Freetown, her contacts with the Christian community proved insufficient for building a stable economic firm. Thus shipping kola directly to the Gambian agents became too risky to continue.

In fact, Palmer and her mother were unable to adapt to the new developments and challenges in the kola trade. At first, continuing to buy their kola from women at Government Wharf, they maintained their contacts with traders along the coastal belt. However, this was an era in which the coastal belt decreased in importance while rail-borne kola flooded the market from the interior. The Lebanese, who had no trouble establishing contacts with other Lebanese traders in The Gambia, controlled this rail-borne trade and pushed Palmer and others like her out of the trade. Although Palmer and her mother had been moderately successful, the greater volume of kola coming into Freetown dictated an increased need for capital in order to remain competitive. Trusted by European firms and banks, many Lebanese traders had greater access to the necessary capital than had Palmer, whose ties to European businesses are conspicuously absent. Thus it became more profitable for Palmer and her mother to sell their kola nuts to the Lebanese who prepared them in large bulk for export.[12]

By 1937, the year of Ruth George's death, Palmer's business had ceased to be profitable. Consequently, she began to rely on her other skills by reestablishing her sewing classes in Freetown and teaching at Buxton Memorial School. Krios have been criticized for forsaking commerce for the professions and thus losing their economic position in Sierra Leone.[13] While this criticism may ring true for some Krios, certainly others must have turned to the professions only after their businesses failed or after it was clear that economic opportunities would be severely limited.

Fortunately Palmer had wisely invested profits from her earlier, more prosperous years by buying Freetown property, and so she was able to live comfortably despite her declining business profits. As far back as the 1790s Krios considered real estate a good investment; Palmer continued the tradition of earlier Krios who looked to property as insurance against the ever-fluctuating economic scene. As added insurance for the future, many Krios invested in

their children's education, recognizing its economic value and expecting that their children would provide for them in old age. In this
regard, Palmer was no exception. She decided to spend her senior
years with the most successful of her three children. Her daughter,
Ruth Luke, is a schoolteacher and a substantial property holder.
The widow of a prominent educator, Luke was influential in Freetown and Sierra Leonean politics in 1977. Having allied herself
closely to the ruling party, the All-Peoples' Congress (APC), Luke
had access to President Siaka Stevens. And as vice-president of the
APC Women's Movement, she worked actively for the government.

In the 1960s, when the recently widowed Luke had the opportunity to travel to Australia for further studies, Palmer moved into
her daughter's house to care for Luke's three children.[14] There
Palmer remained when field research was done in 1977. Although
she had given up her teaching career over twenty years earlier,
Palmer still maintained a small trade in print cloth for Krio-style
dresses. While her daughter would have gladly supported her,
Palmer would never have willingly given up the independence that
her own business afforded.

From her earliest days Palmer had been trained for a life of
commerce. Her apprenticeship at the Big Market and up-country
equipped her with the necessary skills to compete economically in
the early twentieth century. In combination with her formal educational and religious training, her apprenticeship prepared her for a
successful career away from home. Once she embarked on her
eighteen-year stay in The Gambia, she ably demonstrated that she
had acquired both the necessary business acumen and the appropriate attitudes for survival in another country.

On her return to Sierra Leone, however, she was unable to
sustain her business successes in the face of Lebanese competition.
That she and her mother managed to remain prominent in the
kola trade well into the 1930s attests to their skill and determination. Their ultimate failure was the result of their inability to expand into the newly opened interior source of kola. In addition,
Palmer and her mother lacked the necessary capital (or the access
to capital) the new economic order required, and so they were
unable to withstand Lebanese competition. Finally, their business
failed because the basic structure of the Krio diaspora had crum-
bled and been replaced by a foreign minority.

The Krioization of Lillie Mae Domingo

The life of Lillie Mae Domingo (née Wilberforce) illustrates the close ties between interior peoples and settlers. There were several routes indigenous peoples could use to become settlers. Connections to settler society through marriage, trade, education, and religion all helped establish a settler identity. Domingo used all of them as a means of joining Krio society. She was one of the many bridges that enabled commerce to flow within Sierra Leone and between Sierra Leone and the outside world. She understood both cultures and moved easily between them.

By a strict definition of the term, Domingo cannot be called a Krio, for her mother was Afro-American and her father was Mende. But she was considered Krio by virtue of her marriage, education, religion, and occupation. Her Mende grandfather, William Wilberforce, originally came from Imperi and worked at the United Brethren of Christ Mendi Mission in Bonthe as a young man. Domingo described him as "*the* famous William Wilberforce," and he was indeed well known in the context of Sherbro history. He named one of his sons after Dr. Daniel Flickinger, the American missionary who published several books on his experience in Sierra Leone.[15]

The son, Daniel Flickinger Wilberforce, proved to be a bright student. When he was only fourteen he was chosen to accompany a sick missionary back to New York City. When Wilberforce and the missionary arrived in New York, Dr. Flickinger met them at the ship. Immediately taking a liking to his young namesake, Flickinger decided to send Wilberforce to school. Wilberforce attended Steele High School in Dayton, Ohio, where he met Elizabeth Harris; they were married after he completed his schooling.[16]

Daniel Wilberforce returned with his wife to the Shenge Mission on Sierra Leone's Shenge Island, where in 1897 he became the principal of the Rufus Clark and Wife Training School.[17] The Wilberforces had four children: Lillie Mae, born in 1887, was the youngest. Largely because of the Wilberforce family, the U.B.C. mission developed an unusually close relationship with the Sherbro people.[18] Rev. Wilberforce successfully exploited his family ties with the ruling people in Imperi and with the American missionaries. Comfortable among Africans, the British, and Americans, he represented a bridge between the cultures and exerted his influence on political and economic matters. He even had his own soldiers. In 1878 Wilberforce used Imperi soldiers to beat off an attack on the Shenge Mission.[19]

This attack embodied the discomfort of many Sherbro people with his role, for Wilberforce represented a threat to the local authorities. For example, he urged payment of the house tax.[20] When the 1898 war broke out, Wilberforce and his family were not spared. Before the mission was attacked they had to flee to the bush, where they hid until they were rescued by the First West India Regiment on June 15, 1898.[21] Attempting to escape by canoe, his less fortunate mother and sister were caught and killed.[22]

As part of the effort to replace rebel Mende chiefs, the British rewarded Wilberforce for his loyalty by making him chief of Imperi. But after experiencing such great loss in the war and worried about the safety of their children, the Wilberforce family arranged for them to go to school in the United States. As a result, all four children arrived in Dayton, Ohio, in 1901. During the first year in Ohio the children received private tutoring. The following year the three elder children entered Central College in Huntington, Indiana, while Lillie Mae Wilberforce attended the public elementary school in Dayton. After she completed the fifth grade, she and her elder sister, Lucinda, returned to Sierra Leone. Upon their return Lucinda began a career as a teacher and missionary in Freetown, and Domingo entered Wesley Girls' High School to complete her education. The brothers remained longer in the United States and married Afro-Americans before returning home as missionaries.[23]

While in high school in Freetown, Lillie Mae Wilberforce made important contacts within the Krio community and became familiar with the way of life in the capital city. Soon after graduating from high school she completed her entrance into Krio society by marrying Carl Domingo. He had been working as a clerk for the colonial government in Calabar, Nigeria, but had returned home to find a wife. Soon after their August 5, 1910, wedding Carl Domingo took his wife with him to Lagos, where he continued to work for the British colonial government.[24] Although she did not become involved in a large-scale trading network between Sierra Leone and Nigeria as had many wives who followed their husbands to other colonies, Lillie Mae Domingo did begin trading on her own as a prepared-food vendor. Substituting labor and time for her lack of capital, she sold pancakes to workers at the British offices. This small-scale trade brought Domingo a measure of independence and occupied her time while her husband was at work. Because her customers mainly included workers at the colonial offices, trading put Domingo in touch with the Sierra Leonean expatriate community in Nigeria, who were her main source of customers.

In 1914, two years after the Domingos gave birth to their only child Carl, Junior, they returned to Sierra Leone and settled in Bonthe.[25] There Domingo began to trade in earnest. She started as a seamstress, and with the profits from this occupation she purchased cloth from a European factory. Setting up contact with two Krio agents at Torma-Bum on the Bum River, she would send them the cloth which they sold in exchange for palm oil. She would then go to Torma-Bum to collect the palm oil and take it by launch to Freetown. She generally collected about thirty cans of palm oil. In Freetown she sold the oil to marketwomen. With these profits she would buy about five shillings worth of onions at three to five pence for three onions. Returning to Bonthe with these onions, she sold them for about three to five pence per onion.

Domingo learned from her aunt how to trade in kola nuts. The aunt took her into the riverine area and taught her how to collect kola from the farmers. They would return to Bonthe with the kola and sell them to the Compagnie Française de l'Afrique Occidentale (CFAO). Although Domingo never traded in kola on a large scale, she aided other members of her family who did. For example, her first cousin Charlotte Leonard, who lived in Freetown, would arrive in Bonthe just before the kola season began. From there she traveled up the Bum River in search of kola nuts. On her return she would stay with Domingo for about a week, during which time she organized the shipment of the kola to Freetown. In town, she sold her kola to Sierra Leonean women. An aunt who also traded in kola would stay with Domingo, who would arrange her aunt's passage and the shipment of the kola directly to Conakry.[26] Although Domingo had only a limited kola trade of her own, in this way she played an important part in the trading network; her main function was to assist her female relative in making transportation arrangements and to provide them with food and shelter during their stay in Bonthe.

Although Domingo's father was Mende and her mother Afro-American, she had become thoroughly Krioized. Mende women do not have a strong tradition of trading,[27] but Domingo devoted most of her time to this work. Until World War II she continued her own trade in palm oil and onions and assisted her relatives in the kola trade. When age began to slow her down, she returned to selling processed food. She continued this trade until her eyesight deteriorated to nearly total blindness in the mid-1960s. Domingo never rejected her Mende identity. Instead, using contacts on both sides for her economic benefit, she served as a bridge between the two cultures.

Like many other Krio women, she valued education. With her trading profits, she paid the school fees for her son to attend Prince of Wales High School. This education enabled him to get a civil service job. Although he is no longer a member of his mother's church, the U. B. C., Carl Domingo sings in the choir of Holy Trinity Church, one of the more elite Krio churches.[28] Membership in Holy Trinity Church represented a rise to the top of Krio society for the Domingo family.[29]

Lillie Mae Domingo thought of herself as a Krio and wore Krio-style dresses; in addition, she was considered a Krio by the Bonthe community. As such she embraced Krio values and passed them on to her son, who was a fully participating member of Freetown's Krio society. Domingo, in crossing from her own culture into Kriodom, helped establish a channel of communication between the indigenous population, settlers, and Europeans.

The Legend of Abi Jones

Neither Bure Palmer nor Lillie Mae Domingo led extraordinary lives; instead their stories represent the lives of hundreds of settler women who entered trade along the coast. Abigail Charlotte Powells Jones, on the other hand, was a legend in her own time. Establishing a reputation as the queen among Big Market traders, she maintained and expanded one of the largest firms ever run by a Krio woman.

The granddaughter of the Yoruba Recaptive Abarimoko and daughter of a ship pilot, Thomas Powells, Abi Jones was born on May 12, 1868.[30] When her mother died nine years later, Jones and her sister, Hannah, were taken in by a Methodist missionary at the

Female Educational Institute. While living with the missionary, Jones attended Jehovah School and the Government Model School.

Her business training was not ignored, however, for she studied under two of Freetown's most successful Krio traders, her paternal aunts Mary Powells and Jane Powells Mends. From their stalls at the Big Market they founded the Ships Chandlers and General Contractors Company.[31] This company was the result of years of painstaking work building up an extensive network of suppliers of palm produce, vegetables, and fruit. The Powells sisters, among the first traders at the Big Market, brought an already well-developed business to the market. Standing out among women through their contacts with European shipping companies, they established a reputation for reliability.

Abi Jones learned well from her aunts. As the Powells sisters grew older, Abi Jones, her sister Hannah, and her male cousin Hennessey Mends increasingly took control of the business. Eventually they split the company in two when Hennessey Mends went off on his own; Abi Jones ran her half of the business from the Big Market, where she maintained the largest stall in the marketplace.[32] As she took over from the Powells, Jones was careful to keep intact the network of produce suppliers that they had built together. Full of energy, she established close personal relationships with the many carriers who brought produce to her. In addition, she even got to know many of the producers, establishing deals that encouraged her producers to sell their goods exclusively to her. An example of such a supplier was Sarah Cole of Leicester, who sold all her garden vegetables to Jones.[33] Besides close ties with suppliers and carriers, Jones developed relationships with European importers and shippers. Continuing her aunts' reputation for reliability, she was able to gain substantial credit concessions from the European firms. The firms seemed to trust her despite the fact that she was beginning to rival them, for she established direct import and export relations with British, German, and American firms trading in tropical produce or exporting manufactured goods to West Africa.[34]

As a successful merchant, Abi Jones was welcomed into one of the elite Krio families through her marriage to Radcliffe Theophilus Jones, known as Borbor Ajayi. He was the son of John

Thomas Jones, a graduate of Fourah Bay College and a Church Missionary Society catechist in the village of Hastings, and of Mary Ann Lisk, daughter of the Recaptive Obajiri, a sexton of the Anglican Christ Church.[35] Borbor Ajayi worked as a customs officer, but as Abi Jones's business expanded he gave up his civil service position to help out. From their position in the Big Market, they became the major suppliers to Fourah Bay College, Connaught Hospital, and the British troops stationed at Mount Aureol. In addition, they often won contracts to supply many of the ships that docked at Freetown. In 1893, when the West India troops were sent from Freetown to The Gambia to squash the resistance of Fode Silla to British rule,[36] the Joneses sailed up the coast with their provisions.[37] In the late 1890s they began shipping piassava, a coarse fiber used to make brushes, to Britain, Japan, and the United States.[38]

Unfortunately for Abi Jones, she had eleven sons but no daughters to carry on her business. The seven sons who survived infancy served as Abi Jones's apprentices as if they were her daughters, however. From the family's profits three of the sons went to Britain for their education. Upon his return the eldest and most famous son, Dr. Radcliffe Dugan Jones, built a nursing home and offered free treatment to poor people. His humanitarianism was honored in 1953 with a statue in Victoria Park, Freetown. Another son, Percy John Jones, also brought honor to the family when he was made a bishop of the Anglican Church. Although the remaining sons trained for civil service jobs, they continued to help out with the family business.[39]

The Jones family, unlike other Big Market traders, were able to sustain their successes despite Lebanese competition. They did lose their piassava business during the 1940s, but they maintained close ties to their suppliers and continued to supply institutions like Fourah Bay College. When Abi Jones died in 1942, she left her sons a healthy business. Led by their brothers Roland and Teddy Jones, the sons continued the business in the Big Market until 1950. In that year they moved across the street and renamed the business the Jones Brothers of King Jimmy. Although in 1976 they continued to be one of the main produce suppliers to government institutions, by 1980 the business had closed.

As Abi Jones's business grew, her reputation spread throughout

Sierra Leone. Rumors also spread. Some claimed she had "special powers" beyond her business acumen; others claimed she was dishonest.[40] It is certain that she was a dedicated, shrewd woman who worked long hours building up a business network that sustained her family business when others around her were going bankrupt. Abi Jones, the queen of the Big Market traders, deserves her legendary status.

The Collective Portrait

The success of the Jones family firm stands out because it lasted over three generations, beginning in the mid-nineteenth century and still operating in 1977. Her achievements stand in contrast to the modest successes and failures of Bure Palmer and Lillie Mae Domingo. Despite the disparity in accomplishments, four inter-related themes—education, religion, capitalist adaptation, and family—run through the lives of all three.

To understand these women's lives, the concept of education as a western, school-based enterprise must be broken. The apprenticeships Bure Palmer and Abi Jones served in the Big Market were as important as formal schooling in their lives as future traders. As an adult, Domingo had to learn from her aunt how to trade on Sherbro Island despite her long years of Western-style education. Yet clearly the balance of importance was shifting from apprenticeship to formal schooling during these women's lives. Without the skills Palmer had learned at school she would have had very few options after her business failed. In addition, while all assumed that their children would be educated, only Abi Jones trained any of her children for trading. For only the most successful women traders could offer any security for their children's future.

Religion ranked with education as a significant theme in these three biographies. Both Palmer and Domingo emphasized the personal importance of Christianity. When Palmer suffered a mild stroke shortly before Christmas in 1976, many members from her own church, Buxton Memorial, and other Freetown churches came to wish her well. Clearly, she was an intimate member of Freetown's Christian community. For Palmer, and especially for Domingo, education and religious training were combined. For Domingo, they prepared her for a life as a Krio. Attendance at Wesleyan

Girls' High School and connections to the United Brethren of Christ were crucial elements in her new identity.

The centrality of Christianity in Palmer and Domingo's lives reflects its growing influence among non-Muslim Krios in the twentieth century.[41] Neither of these women mentioned the influence of indigenous religions or secret societies in their lives. Their biographies raise questions about the role of Christian churches in creating both ethnic identity and class cohesion. As is suggested by the experience of Lillie Mae Domingo's son Carl, Junior, the elite Anglican and Methodist churches distinguished their members from most of Freetown's inhabitants and helped establish petit bourgeois credentials. Did a non-Muslim Krio woman have to be a Christian to remain in good standing in the Krio community? Abigail Jones's life history suggests that this was not necessarily the case. Although she may have been religious, no informants spoke of her in such terms. They were more concerned with her business acumen and her possession of "special powers." Nonetheless, prestige was brought to her entire family when her son Percy Jones became an Anglican bishop. The weakness of her Christian identity may reflect the fact that Jones's life seems more like a throwback to the nineteenth century. Her life-style, continuing connections to non-Krio producers, and her very economic success were clearly unusual for the mid-twentieth century.

Contrasted with Domingo and Palmer's trading experiences Jones's successes illustrate the difficulties Krio women faced in adapting to an era of capitalist expansion—the third common theme of this collective portrait. Domingo and Palmer lacked the access to capital that a trader needed to succeed during the 1900s. When Domingo traded palm oil for onions in Freetown and sold those onions in Bonthe, she made almost a 200 percent profit. But her initial capital was so small that even a 200 percent profit did not permit her to accumulate much capital. Similarly, the moderate capital from Palmer's joint venture with her mother was insufficient to withstand competition from the Lebanese who had greater access to capital and who drove them out of business.[42]

In contrast, Abigail Jones successfully moved from being a trader to being a businesswoman who headed a family firm. The development of family firms aids capital accumulation. Increased capital gave Jones the advantages Palmer and Domingo lacked and

put her in a class with Lebanese traders. With capital, she was able
to maintain her supply network. Although her relationship to suppliers was based on social as well as economic factors, she could not
have sustained such an extensive network without offering the
suppliers economic advantages. Other Krio women found that suppliers with whom they had long-standing partnerships abandoned
them for Lebanese traders. Operating on the grand scale of a
family firm and maintaining ties to her loyal producers, Jones was
able to buy large quantities of goods in the manner of Lebanese
traders. Her strong, dominating personality held this firm together
through three generations. Therefore, unlike most other Krio
women, she not only survived but diversified her business into such
areas as exporting piassava.

Mere maintenance of a firm founded by women for over a hundred years was a major achievement. The incorporation of male
members of the family into the business was a step toward expansion. The major limitation of this family firm lay in its inability to
incorporate outsiders (i.e., accountants, specialists, clerks, etc.) and
thereby grow even further. Given the economic obstacles that all
African merchants faced during the colonial era, this failure to
expand was not surprising. After the end of colonialism, the firm
had passed its most successful days and the two sons most involved
in the trade were unable to make it grow to the point where outsiders would have been necessary. Indeed, the death of Abi Jones
in 1942 marked the end of an era dominated by an unusual twentieth-century Krio woman trader who combined extraordinary
commercial skill with capital.

Inseparable from the themes of education, religion, and capitalist adaptation is the issue of the family relations that helped
organize these women's lives. While men influenced their lives
somewhat, these women were raised in female-centered families.
Aunts seemed to be at least as important to them as mothers in
passing on trading skills. For Lillie Mae Domingo these relatives
were essential, since her mother came from outside the culture and
did not engage in trading. All the women continued the practice of
their aunts by basing their trade on family ties. Trading networks
were in large part kinship networks. Only Abi Jones successfully established enduring connections outside of her family to

spread her economic influence throughout the peninsula and its hinterland.

Despite this reliance on women's networks, all three had remarkably stable marriages. None followed the nineteenth-century pattern of trading in a residence separate from their husbands. Both Palmer and Domingo followed their husbands to their jobs in other colonies. Their lives seemed partially constrained by the standards of Christian marriage. As usual, Abi Jones's life seemed to be from an earlier century. According to informants, she headed her houshold despite her husband's presence.[43]

Finally these three biographies are stories of adaptation to the vicissitudes of Sierra Leone's political economy. In 1977 Palmer and Domingo were spirited women despite old age and illness. They projected a sense of self-worth and pride for lives well lived. Abi Jones's legend speaks across the decades of a woman with similar attributes. Unravelng the threads of their lives from the web of Krio women's history reveals the power of that history.

Chapter 5
Krio Women Traders in Historical and Comparative Perspective

Much of the writing on West African women has clearly delineated the active role they have played in their economies as they expanded from agricultural and domestic roles into trade. Most of this literature has focused on the impact of the growing world economy on these women's status. One view stresses the advantages women derived from the Afro-European trade. The strongest work in this school of thought was written before the 1970s and thus before theories of underdevelopment came to affect most writing on African history. These works also tend to be uninfluenced by feminist writings on African women, but they serve as models to be criticized by later writers. Moreover, this literature continues to shed important light on the changing status of African women. The basic argument of such writers as Robert LeVine, Niara Sudarkasa, and Phoebe Ottenberg is that expanding economic opportunities led to increased economic independence for women.[1] As LeVine puts it,

> under European administration, with the establishment of internal peace and the development of overseas trade, marketing activities increased, offering new opportunities to women as well as men. In some areas, these opportunities augmented the mobility and economic autonomy of women, causing drastic changes in the husband-wife relationship.[2]

LeVine draws on three examples to support this statement. Using Nadel's work on the Nupe,[3] he suggests that under British rule an increasing number of married women engaged in long-distance trade. This represented a change from precolonial days when long-distance trading was generally limited to childless women, "where sexual laxity while away from their husbands was regarded as permissible."[4] As a consequence of their increased economic activities, women began contributing a larger share of the family income than did their poor, farming husbands.[5]

LeVine draws his second example from Ottenberg's work on the Afikpo Igbo.[6] Focusing on the positive impact of British rule on Afikpo women, Ottenberg maintains that there was

> ... a marked increase in physical mobility as a result of the cessation of the slave trade and inter-group warfare, an increase in resources with a consequent rise in the standard of living, and a growth in the economic independence of women.[7]

These changes resulted, in part, from women's acceptance of cassava as a subsistence and cash crop, for it alleviated the famine that generally preceded the harvest of the traditional male crop, the yam, and brought increased income to women who sold their cassava surplus.

Finally, LeVine illustrates the positive effects of European rule, presenting his own research on Yoruba women. Reflecting Yorubaland's well-developed economy, these famous traders have engaged in long-distance trade for centuries. Two major works on Yoruba women by Hodder and Sudarkasa support LeVine's position that despite the long history of their trading, European contact has increased economic opportunities for women. Sudarkasa, for example, maintains that "although their employment in trade predates the era of the Pax Britannica, the twentieth-century expansion of the market economy has led to an expansion in the range and scale of their activities."[8]

This argument was challenged in the 1970s by scholars who suggested that it neglected the negative economic impact of European contact on African women.[9] For instance, Sidney Mintz, in an early and influential piece, has argued that since the imposition of colonial rule the economic position of women has eroded vis-à-vis that of men.[10] He bases his argument on the theory articulated by Paul Bohannon and George Dalton that capitalist penetration into African economies led to a decline in importance of markets, the major site of women's economic activity.[11] Thus while internal marketing systems may have expanded to serve growing urban areas and nonagricultural labor forces, economic transactions not readily negotiated in markets also expanded. Women who worked at markets, the center of economic activity during the precolonial era, found themselves restricted to these areas in the colonial era, when Africa was drawn more closely into the world capitalist system. This limitation adversely affected women because the expansion of opportunities within the internal marketing system lagged behind economic developments in other parts of the economy. Consequently, Mintz argues, economic developments following European domination eroded the position of women relative to men even though petty trading opportunities may have increased. The reasons for this erosion were complex. First, women were surpassed economically by men who both invaded their stronghold, the markets, and expanded into new economic opportunities that largely excluded women, such as trading with European firms.[12] Second, women lost independence when they moved into low status, salaried jobs, since men often gained control over their income.[13]

A number of case studies were published during the 1970s that lend support to Mintz's arguments. For example, Leith Mullings discusses Mintz's hypotheses and presents her study of the Ga women of Labadi, Ghana, as supporting his conclusions.[14] Influenced both by underdevelopment theory and emerging feminist analysis of women's status, she argues that "the acceleration of class stratification under colonialism resulted in the deterioration of the position of women relative to that of men."[15] According to Mullings, the Labadi women, responding to new economic opportunities, turned enthusiastically from farming to petty trade. Women traded their husbands' fish and produce, and consequently they had greater access to cash than the husbands. But Mullings also says that this depiction of the situation leaves the false impression that women's position had improved relative to their husbands'. In fact, women's relative economic strength had declined for three reasons. First, women were alienated from the land because traditional patterns of communal land ownership were disrupted. As land became more valuable, men who held the land in the name of the community began to claim private ownership.

Second, women were limited to petty trading opportunities, selling low value items such as agricultural goods, cloth, and canned foods. Few found jobs in the emerging industrial sectors. Thus they were restricted to precarious, time-consuming work that generally yielded small profits to a few women while many were plunged into debt. Third, the increasing number of monogamous marriages among the Labadi isolated women from each other, limiting their ability to share domestic duties. Women in monogamous marriages were more likely to be deterred by their husbands from making an independent living than those in polygynous marriages.

Finally, Labadi women suffered a loss in political power. In precolonial days the *manyei* (mother of the town), who represented women, was one of many officers holding political power. But during the colonial era the traditional arrangement was disrupted when one of the political officers, the *mantse* (the father of the town), was treated by the British as the "chief" among the Ga. Subsequently the mantse gained in political power while the office of manyei became almost extinct.[16]

Mullings concludes:

> As land became a commodity, political power, formerly diffuse, became concentrated in the hands of the colonialist and to a lesser extent, the chief and a few elders. This development had particularly negative results for women, especially since it appears to have been accompanied by the decline of their . . . vehicles of traditional power. Although women's access to the marketplace gives the appearance of improved status, especially where the majority of men are farmers and fishermen, I suggest that this improvement in status is illusory. As long as women's access to all non-traditional sectors of the economy remains limited, their traditional hegemony is doomed to ultimate deterioration as industrialized, stratified society replaces the traditional village community.[17]

Mullings touches on the loss of political power by Labadi women. Two other influential writers, both studying Igbo women, focus on this loss in power and, in the process, have contributed to the growing feminist analysis of women's status.[18] Kamene Okonjo maintains that before colonialism Igbo societies were organized as "dual-sex" systems in which "each sex manages its own affairs, and women's interests are represented at all levels."[19] At the head of the female side of this system was the *omu*: her duties included supervising the community market, handling husband/wife disputes, and overseeing title-taking by women. When the British established colonial rule and attempted to rule through "established" rulers, their "single-sex" heritage in which males dominated the political sphere made them blind to the power women held among the Igbo. Therefore the British elevated the male monarch, the *obi*, while they ignored the female monarch, the omu. The omu, consequently, lost her traditional power base. Now women as well as men were responsible to the obi. In addition, the omu lost control over the markets as imported goods disrupted her system of price-fixing and her "market medicines" became obsolete. Finally, Christianity pulled women away from their desire to obtain titles. Thus, "the *omu* lost her prestige and her clientele as her political and religious functions were replaced by colonial rule and Christianity."[20]

Judith Van Allen has also addressed herself to Igbo women's loss of political power, but she focuses on the Igbo "Women's War." Like Okonjo, Van Allen feels that the British, with their Victorian beliefs, were blind "to the possibility that women had had a significant role in traditional politics. . . ."[21] Political power among the Igbo was diffuse; and women's political power was based on their group meetings (*mitiri*), market networks, kinship groups, and right to use boycotts and force to effect their decisions. When the British tried to build colonial rule upon indigenous male-dominated institutions, they weakened women's traditional autonomy and power without providing alternative forms of power and autonomy. Igbo women responded to this loss in power by using their traditional power bases, and the Igbo Women's War resulted.

The women struck out against the most visible sign of their grievances, the British-established warrant chiefs and native courts who abused the immunity stemming from their privileged position by harrassing women. The women attacked the warrant chiefs in 1929, organized through their market networks. The British restored order, but not until sixty women lay dead. Despite an intensive investigation in which the British discovered the market network used to organize the war, the colonial administration never understood the true nature of the women's grievances, for it was incomprehensible to them that they had contributed to women's loss of power and status in West Africa.

Examination of Sierra Leone's settler women sheds light on the controversy over the impact of colonial rule on African women. In Sierra Leone, the British never knew quite what to make of the settler women. They were obviously disturbed by the way Sierra Leonean women grabbed the economic opportunities opened up by the colony's foundation. Nova Scotian, Maroon, and Liberated African women were all by-products of the Atlantic slave trade. Their emergence in the economic drama taking place on the Upper Guinea coast symbolized both the growing control that Northwestern Europe was establishing over West Africa and the movement inland of the Afro-European frontier. Unwittingly these women, along with other coastal economic intermediaries, introduced into African economies the beginning of a new European hegemony. From the beginning, settler women were closely tied to the evolving world capitalist system, and they were innovative in the pursuit of their economic interests. But they had little control over events. In the 1850s they demonstrated their economic power by convincing the colonial administration to build the Big Market, while the big male traders, both African and European, negotiated to keep import duties low and export duties nonexistent.[22]

The settlers' economic decline in the twentieth century demonstrated how minimal was the settler women's control over events. The late nineteenth-century economic depression, provincial hostility, Lebanese competition, and British enmity combined to obstruct the settlers' development into an independent bourgeoisie. Most importantly, the exigencies of British colonial rule dictated that these economic and cultural intermediaries be moved out of trade. These were factors faced by all Krios, male and female. Because Krio women were generally less well off than Krio men, however, they suffered more from this economic decline and loss of mobility. As Krio women moved away from independent trading they lost some of the economic reinforcement they had had for their independent life-styles. Beyond the economic pressures to give up commerce was the insistence of their husbands that they remain at home. The need to build a tighter ethnic identity was not compatible with physical mobility. The impact of the ethnic rivalry fostered by the extension of colonial rule to the protectorate forced many women home and into a more dependent relationship with their husbands. Colonialism, which at one time had opened up economic opportunities for Nova Scotian and Liberated African women, now contributed to a loss of economic opportunities for these same women. Maroon women, having started out relatively disadvantaged, experienced little change in status.

The issue has further complexities. Because of the long tradition of missionary education, Krio women had more alternatives to petty trade than most African women. Some were able to turn to the professions despite traditional British hostility to female participation. Present-day Krios are proud of the number of women who have become lawyers and doctors or entered other professions that are normally restricted to men. Nonetheless, most have been restricted to professions traditionally dominated by women—i.e., nursing, clerical work, and high school teaching. But whether the move from trading to salaried positions was negative for Krio women, as Mintz and Mullings would imply, must be questioned. Granted, when women moved into traditionally female positions they were at a disadvantage with respect to their husbands, who had greater mobility in male-dominated professions. Nonetheless, salaried occupations offered women both an alternative to the harsh life of petty trading and a degree of security. Both Mintz and Mullings lament the loss of independence that goes with this change, but they must have forgotten what life was like for a petty trader who barely made ends meet, or even for more prosperous traders who were always threatened with bankruptcy.

Education and salaried jobs offered Krio women positive alternatives to their declining economic status.[23] Bure Palmer's autobiography illustrates this point. When her kola/groundnut trade with The Gambia collapsed, Palmer turned to the skills she had learned in mission schools to sustain herself. Because she was female, perhaps she was barred from the higher-paying government jobs men might fill. Nonetheless, teaching provided her with a more secure income than she could have obtained from trading.

In the political arena, the settler women were at a disadvantage from the founding of Sierra Leone, because its political structure was created by British colonizers who tended to limit women's direct access to political power. As Okonjo observes, the British system was based on a single-sex heritage in which males dominated the political sphere. Under such a system, "women can achieve recognition and distinction only by taking on the roles of men in public life and performing them well."[24] And, as Van Allen implies, British men were not prepared to recognize an active political role for African women.[25]

Nova Scotian women had arrived in Africa prepared to participate in the political life of the new colony, but the Sierra Leone Company decided in 1797 to take the vote away from women.[26] Not until they participated in their first municipal election in 1930 did Krio women regain the right to vote.[27] Because the British never recognized women's legitimate claim to active political participation, they never appointed women to the legislative council, the only formal avenue open for participation by the colonized. When Constance Cummings-John became the first woman in West Africa to be elected to a town council, in 1938, however, some people hoped that she would be nominated for the legislative council.[28] But this wish never became a reality. Moreover, Cummings-John was an exceptional woman who achieved distinction and recognition in a traditionally male role. Her participation in the political arena, while symbolizing increased political participation of women, did not represent their collective emergence on an equal footing with men.

Colonialism did not necessarily signal a complete decline for all women in Sierra Leone. Enterprising provincial women, although prevented from entering intermediary positions by Lebanese dominance of this sector, filled a vacuum that the economic decline of Krio women traders created. Thus the impact of colonialism was complex. All women traders were now more restricted to petty trading; but the Krio women's decline during the late colonial era opened up trading opportunities for some provincial women.

The history of Sierra Leone's settler women is a history of implicit class formation. In the nineteenth century settler women were not distinguished by marked class distinctions. A few women may have been considered elite by virtue of marriage to elite men and their Westernized life-style. Most, however, were petty traders, only a small number of whom advanced to larger scale trade. With the advent of twentieth-century changes, class differences among Krio women became more apparent. Women had differential access to education and salaried and professional jobs. While family ties mitigated against class differentiation, distinctions did exist. For example, it was those women who were most exposed to Western-style education, such as Cummings-John, who had political influence.

Women brought different backgrounds to the colonial experience and responded to it based in part on their cultural roots and class position. Those such as LeVine and Ottenberg, who argue for the positive impact of colonial rule, and those such as Mintz and Mullings, who argue the opposite, make a crucial error in viewing gender as a monolithic, independent variable. In part, this error stems from the misguided attempt to isolate one variable, such as mode of production, as affecting all women the same way. Such attempts are doomed to failure because of their overly narrow view of what contributes to women's status. It is not sufficient to look at the economic forces in women's lives while ignoring the impact of religion, ideology, and kinship relations. Nor should women be seen as an undifferentiated mass with the same opportunities and constraints.

Women as Cultural Brokers?

In addition to their role as traders, settler women played a role as cultural intermediaries. The history of the women traders reveals several dimensions of this intermediary role. As active participants in the economic drama, settler women sought out this role. They emerged from the indigenous peoples to intermarry with the settler community and thus ease the strangers' introduction into Sierra Leone. These women joined with Liberated Africans and Nova Scotian women to help uphold the emerging traditions of Kriodom. Big Market traders, for instance, combined Christian ideas with African religious beliefs to form a uniquely Krio world view. Yet unlike many other settler women (e.g., Hausa women in Yoruba towns), Krio women did not remain tied to their own group, for they also crossed ethnic boundaries to join with the indigenous peoples and thus further facilitate cross-cultural contact.

Conspicuously absent from the literature on culture contact and ethnic boundaries is a discussion of women as cultural intermediaries. Most of the literature, when it does recognize a female role, presents a picture of women as pawns moved about in marriage alliances for the convenience of men.[29] What women did once they married and the other intermediary roles they filled generally go unnoticed.

Exceptions exist. For example, the literature on the *signares* of the Senegambia presents women as motivated, active participants in an economic drama.[30] Almost as soon as Europeans began trading along the West African coast they formed social and economic ties with coastal women. In the Senegambia the Europeans, largely Portuguese at first, were called *lancados* for having thrown themselves among the Africans.[31] The women with whom the lancados formed unions were known as signares in Senegal, *nhara* in Portuguese Guinea, and *senora* in The Gambia.[32] Generally Wolof, Lebou, or Eurafrican, these women became famous for the wealth and political power they amassed. By cohabiting with the European traders, the signares were able to collaborate with foreigners for their mutual economic benefit, for the women brought with them ties to the indigenous population and the men ties to commercial firms in Europe.

By the middle of the eighteenth century, the signares of Saint-Louis had accumulated great wealth, which they were able to sustain through many changes in European colonial rulers. Their wealth was represented best by the numerous slaves and clients whom they controlled. Florence Mahoney asserts that in the eighteenth century, next to the Europeans, "the *Senoras* were the most prosperous, owning substantial houses, and wielding considerable influence in society as heads of enormous households of dependents."[33] This influence was social as well as cultural, pulling the European settlers into the cultural realm of African society. While the signares learned certain aspects of Western culture, such as European dances and languages, they enforced African marriage customs, and thus the settler-signare relationship took on a distinctly African flavor.[34] Moreover, European men had to rely on the signares for their survival. Given the harsh realities they faced in precolonial West Africa, Europeans received invaluable services from the signares, including companionship with women at least partially familiar with their languages and culture, stable homelife, meals, and recreational outlets. These services helped maintain the Europeans' psychological as well as physical health.[35]

George Brooks aptly summarizes the significance of the signares:

> Signareship represented an economic nexus between European
> men pursuing personal gain (usually illegally) and African and
> Eurafrican women determined to acquire European merchan-
> dise. It was the women who provided access to African commer-
> cial networks, furnished households with skilled domestic slaves,
> and proved indispensable as interpreters of African languages
> and cultures. In short, *signares* skillfully manipulated two trad-
> ing complexes and cultures to further their own ends. Yet sig-
> nareship represented a social nexus, too, and *signares* helped
> create a way of life, an ambiance, that went far beyond the
> economic relationship. Once the process was well begun, it was
> so advantageous and attractive to all involved, at least in Senegal,
> that it became self-perpetuating. The two societies, Senegalese
> and French, partially blending, largely coexisting, created a
> complex cultural relationship that transcends facile explanation
> or analysis.[36]

Thus the signares provide an example of women as cultural intermediaries easing the contact between the alien Europeans and indigenous Africans. But the signares are only directly comparable to
those Sierra Leonean women who came from the indigenous
culture to fuse with the black settlers. Thus women like Lillie Mae
Domingo clearly perceived the advantages of adopting settler identity and marrying into Krio society. There were numerous opportunities for indigenous women to marry settler men and to establish trading careers or have daughters follow trading careers.
These women opened up the secrets of indigenous culture to a
black settler community and, in turn, introduced elements of settler society into their own.

But what of the settler women who married indigenous men?
Where in the literature is there a comparable example of settler
women embracing indigenous culture? Indeed the literature does
not seem to recognize this role for women as they are generally
presented as upholders of cultural integrity for settler society.

Abner Cohen, for example, maintains that ethnic groups result
from the tendency for men to marry within their own loosely defined ethnic categories. Viewing this development from the per-

spective of the men, he contends that they will become an endog-
amous group or "a group of men who neither give women to
members of other ethnic groups, nor take women from them."[37]
Through their control over the exchange of women, these men
even conspire to limit women to marriage within the group. Thus
endogamy leads to intensive social action within the group and
inhibits interaction with outsiders. Women, Cohen argue, ensure
the stability of communities.[38] Thus among the Hausa in Yoruba
towns there existed a strong prejudice against marriage between
Hausa men and Yoruba women. Since Yoruba women could pull
their Hausa husbands into Yoruba society, intermarriage was
viewed as detrimental to Hausa ethnic exclusiveness, political autonomy, and economic interests. Moreover, the loyalty not only of
the husbands but also of their children became suspect, since the
children's allegiances might be ambivalent. Thus Hausa women
differed from Sierra Leone's settler women in the nineteenth century in that they helped to cement the Hausa's ethnic identity. In
the twentieth century, the Krio women's role, however reluctantly
played, was much more like their Hausa counterparts' because
ethnic identity became a more serious issue than in the earlier
century.

Cohen's discussion of the importance of women in ethnic group
formation is complemented by the literature on settler societies
where women are absent. As Philip Curtin argues, the European
men in Senegambia became closely involved in African society because they had no European women to help them recreate a model
of Western societies.[39] Instead, the society that the European men
created became increasingly African. The offspring of the Europeans and signares were racially and culturally mixed; and third-
and fourth-generation Eurafricans were even further removed
from European culture and tended to merge with the general African population.[40]

The Africanization process of lancados in the Senegambia was
repeated among the Mozambican *prazeros* (holders of titles to Portuguese crown estates). Allen and Barbara Isaacman have given the
most insightful view of this process.[41] By emphasizing the internal
dynamics of the prazeros, they "redefine the *prazeros* as an African
institution operating in its Zambesian milieu."[42] The prazeros, like
the lancados, were what Curtin, in a personal communication to

the Isaacmans, termed transfrontiermen: "people who cross the frontier of their own culture area, often taking up a new way of life."[43] Transfrontier settlers differ from normal frontier settlers in that their core institutions and values are transformed into those of the indigenous culture. "As such, acculturation was substitutive rather than additive, and differed from the process of hybridization which characterized many frontier societies."[44]

A few Portuguese women were included among the prazeros, and efforts were made to restrict their marriage to Portuguese men. For example, in 1755 legislation was passed reconfirming the responsibility of the women to marry Portuguese men.[45] But such legislation passed in faraway Lisbon had little impact on prazero life, and the women, unwilling to marry unsuitable Portuguese men or indigenous men, often married Goans.[46] While this arrangement added to the breakdown of the Portuguese settler community, the number of such women was small. And it was the general absence of women that contributed most to the disintegration of the Portuguese community, for "the lack of European women in the transfrontier community reinforced its cultural isolation and facilitated incorporation into the indigenous society."[47] Thus while frontier settlers are connected to their homeland and within the settler community by kinship networks, transfrontier settlers, because they marry indigenous women, become connected to the host culture.[48]

It would seem, therefore, that the presence of women in a settler community can help cement that community. Clearly Sierra Leone's settler women aided in the formation of settler society. They raised their children in the newly established colony traditions, adhered to the emerging life-style first of women traders and then of women professionals, and participated in colony organizations such as the hunting society with their men. In addition, marriage unions, however loose they may have been, connected settler men and women to the colony.

Yet Sierra Leone's settler women did more than uphold the cultural integrity of Krio society. Although most came from the settler community rather than the indigenous peoples, they acted as cultural intermediaries. Because of the unsettled conditions of nineteenth-century Sierra Leone and the diverse origins of its settler population, women had an unusual amount of freedom of choice in selecting marriage partners. Taking advantage of this opportunity, settler women made connections both within the colony and to the hinterland.

A search through the literature on settler societies in Africa suggests that nineteenth-century Sierra Leonean women were unusual. As cultural intermediaries they eased the contact between Europeans and indigenous societies. As economic intermediaries they assisted the flow of commodities between societies that had very little in common. The central dilemma in assessing their role on the Afro-European frontier lies in the contradictory images that emerge from the part they played in the economic drama. On the one hand, they project an image of women who faced the cruel disruptions of enslavement but managed to piece together a life that took advantage of the economic opportunities presented. In the nineteenth century they traded with relative freedom, and they actively shaped a marriage institution that supported a remarkable degree of autonomy. When they lost much of this freedom in the twentieth century, they fell back on the skills that they learned in schools and prepared themselves to take advantage of the Western-style opportunities available to them.

On the other hand, the negative image that emerges from their history is of women who eased the way for colonial rule in Sierra Leone and its hinterland. In this picture, Krio women appear as unwitting collaborators who did not question the wisdom of working with the British until it was too late; capitalism and colonial rule had been strengthened, and all suffered deprivation and alienation as a result. These contradictory images emerge from the same history. Indeed, the tensions between them reflect the complexities of settler women's lives. A new breed of women, they could not completely control events. They could, and did, survive.

Notes

Chapter 1

1. E. G. Ingham, *Sierra Leone After a Hundred Years* (London: Seely and Co., 1894), pp. 316–17.

2. In 1844, in his report on the Sierra Leone Colony to the governor of Trinidad, R. Guppy maintained that the settlers were "universally considered as an idle and worthless class" because they preferred petty trading to manual labor. The Yoruba Recaptives, while "more provident" and "more desirous of gain" than the Nova Scotians, also preferred trading to "actual labor." Parliamentary Papers (hereafter cited as PP), vol. 52, 1844, p. 322. Later the 1881 census report complained about the large number of colony people, including many women, who were involved in trade rather than the more uplifting farm labor. Report of the Census of Sierra Leone and Its Dependencies Taken in 1881, G3.A1/L114, Church Missionary Society Records, London (hereafter cited as CMS).

3. David Skinner and Barbara E. Harrell-Bond, "Misunderstandings Arising from the Use of the Term 'Creole' in the Literature on Sierra Leone," *Africa* 47, no. 3 (1977): 305–20.

4. For a discussion of the term *Krio*, see C. Magbaily Fyle, *The History of Sierra Leone: A Concise Introduction* (London: Evans Brothers, 1981), p. 73.

5. Christopher Fyfe, "Reform in West Africa: The Abolition of the Slave Trade," in *History of West Africa*, ed. J. F. A. Ajayi and Michael Crowder, vol. 2 (New York: Columbia University Press, 1972), p. 35.

6. Krio women were far from the first women to trade in the area. Among the most fascinating of the early women traders was the Eurafrican Bibiana Vez, who controlled much of the trade between the Gambia and Sierra Leone rivers around the 1670s and 1680s. She also held a Portuguese captain-major hostage for fourteen months and founded an ephemeral state. See George E. Brooks, Jr., "The *Signares* of Saint-Louis and Gorée: Women Entrepreneurs in Eighteenth-Century Senegal," in

Women in Africa: Studies in Social and Economic Change, ed. Nancy Hafkin and Edna Bay (Stanford: Stanford University Press, 1976), p. 20; and Walter Rodney, *A History of the Upper Guinea Coast, 1545 to 1800* (London: Oxford University Press, 1970), pp. 209–10.

7. They rarely competed on the same scale as Krio men, who always outnumbered them in the hinterland trade. This does not mean, however, that they should be ignored, for social historiography attempts to counterbalance the tendency of historians to study only the people with power. Cf. E. J. Hobsbawm, "From Social History to the History of Society," *Daedalus* 100, no. 1 (1971): 20–45; and Martin Klein, "The Decolonization of West African History," *Journal of Interdisciplinary History* 6, no. 1 (1975): 111–25.

8. John D. Hargraves, *A Life of Sir Samuel Lewis* (London: Oxford University Press, 1958).

9. Winwood Reade, *The African Sketch-Book,* vol. 2 (London: Smith, Elder and Co., 1873), p. 399.

10. For a discussion of trading networks in general, see Philip D. Curtin, *Economic Change in Precolonial Africa: Senegambia in the Era of the Slave Trade* (Madison: University of Wisconsin Press, 1975); and idem, *Cross-Cultural Trade in World History* (London: Cambridge University Press, 1984).

11. Cf. Brooks, "*Signares* of Saint-Louis." This articles demonstrates the way in which African and Eurafrican women actively sought out trading opportunities with European traders and administrators by forming marriage alliances with them. The *signares* will be discussed in further detail in chap. 5, as their history offers several points that can be usefully compared to Krio women's trading history.

12. Christopher Fyfe, *A History of Sierra Leone* (London: Oxford University Press, 1962), pp. 244, 351, 455; I. C. Hotobah-During, interview with author, November 25, 1976; Judy Vincent, interview with author, May 5, 1976.

13. For exceptions to this critique, see Barbara Harrell-Bond, Allen Howard, and David Skinner, *Community Leadership and the Transformation of Freetown (1801–1976)* (The Hague: Mouton Publishers, 1978); and John Peterson, *Province of Freedom: A History of Sierra Leone, 1787–1870* (London: Faber and Faber, 1969).

14. Frederik Barth, "Introduction," in *Ethnic Groups and Boundaries: The Social Organization of Culture Difference,* ed. Frederik Barth (Boston: Little, Brown and Co., 1969), p. 10.

15. Cf. Jesse Lemise, "The American Revolution Seen from the Bottom Up," in *Toward a New Past: Dissenting Essays in American History,* ed. Barton J. Bernstein (New York: Pantheon Books, 1968).

16. Hargraves, *Life of Sir Samuel Lewis.*

17. It is not being argued that biographies of elites are invalid ap-

proaches to history, but that when describing the wider society the biographer should not assume that the elite perspective reflects the total culture. When Hargraves views Freetown through the limited perspective of Lewis and his fellow male elites, he gives no indication that other perspectives existed. Thus Hargraves does not place Lewis's life fully within the context of the times and the surrounding society.

18. James W. St. G. Walker, *The Black Loyalists: The Search for a Promised Land in Nova Scotia and Sierra Leone, 1783–1870* (New York: Africana Publishing Co., 1976); Ellen Gibson Wilson, *The Loyal Blacks* (New York: G. P. Putnam's Sons, 1976).

19. Walker, *The Black Loyalists*, pp. 318–19.

20. Wilson, *The Loyal Blacks*, p. 214.

21. See Abner Cohen, *Custom and Politics in Urban Africa: A Study of Hausa Migrants in Yoruba Towns* (Berkeley: University of California Press, 1969), for a discussion of the function of retribalization.

22. Peter H. Wood, "'It was a Negro Taught Them': A Look at African Labor in Early South Carolina," *Journal of Asian and African Studies* 9, nos. 3–4 (1974): 160–79; Walker, *The Black Loyalists*, p. 5. See also Peter Wood, *Black Majority: Negroes in Colonial South Carolina from 1670 through the Stono Rebellion* (New York: W. W. Norton and Co., 1975).

23. Wood, "It was a Negro," p. 172.

24. Ibid.

25. Walker, *The Black Loyalists*, p. 196. Apparently Walker was not familiar with the most recent research on eighteenth-century black families that suggests that marriage bonds were not as "loose" as he proposed. Despite the harsh realities of slave life, Afro-Americans established stable marriage bonds. See Herbert G. Gutman, *The Black Family in Slavery and Freedom, 1750–1925* (New York: Vintage Books, 1977), pp. 11–28.

26. Skinner and Harrell-Bond, "Misunderstandings," 305–20.

27. Ibid., p. 314.

28. See Arthur T. Porter, *Creoledom: A Study of the Development of Freetown Society* (Oxford: Oxford University Press, 1963).

29. For more on Western influences, see Leo Spitzer, *The Creoles of Sierra Leone: Responses to Colonialism, 1870–1949* (Madison: University of Wisconsin Press, 1974).

30. John Peterson, "The Sierra Leone Creole: A Reappraisal," in *Freetown: A Symposium*, ed. Christopher Fyfe and Eldred Jones (Freetown: University of Sierra Leone Press, 1968).

31. Cf. Hargraves, *Life of Sir Samuel Lewis*.

32. See Peterson, *Province of Freedom*.

33. Abner Cohen, "The Politics of Ritual Secrecy," *Man* 6 (1971): 427–48.

34. Spitzer, *Creoles of Sierra Leone*, pp. 4, 15–16.

35. B. W. Hodder and U. J. Ukwu, *Markets in West Africa* (Ibadan, Nigeria: Ibadan University Press, 1969); Niara Sudarkasa, *Where Women Work: A Study of Yoruba Women in the Marketplace and in the Home* (Ann Arbor: University of Michigan, 1973); Robert A. LeVine, "Sex Roles and Economic Change in Africa," in *Black Africa: Its Peoples and Cultures Today*, ed. John Middleton (London: Macmillan and Co., 1970), pp. 174–80.

36. Karen Sacks, *Sisters and Wives: The Past and Future of Sexual Equality* (Urbana: University of Illinois Press, 1982).

37. Frederick Engels, *The Origin of the Family, Private Property and the State* (New York: International Publishers, 1942).

38. Cf. Martin King Whyte, *The Status of Women in Preindustrial Societies* (Princeton: Princeton University Press, 1978), pp. 1–27.

39. Michelle Z. Rosaldo, "Woman, Culture, and Society: A Theoretical Overview," in *Woman, Culture, and Society*, ed. Michelle Z. Rosaldo and Louise Lamphere (Stanford: Stanford University Press, 1974), pp. 17–42.

40. Sherry B. Ortner and Harriet Whitehead, "Introduction: Accounting for Sexual Meanings," in *Sexual Meanings: The Cultural Construction of Gender and Sexuality*, ed. Sherry B. Ortner and Harriet Whitehead (Cambridge: Cambridge University Press, 1981). They also relate this position to the nature/culture opposition articulated by Ortner in 1974. See "Is Female to Male as Nature is to Culture?" in *Woman, Culture, and Society*, ed. Michelle Z. Rosaldo and Louise Lamphere (Stanford: Stanford University Press, 1974), pp. 67–87.

41. For a similar argument, see Niara Sudarkasa, "Female Employment and Family Organization in West Africa," in *The Black Woman Cross-Culturally*, ed. Filomina Chioma Steady (Cambridge Mass.: Schenkman Publishing Co., 1981), pp. 49–63.

42. Cf. Kamene Okonjo, "Women's Political Participation in Nigeria," in *The Black Woman Cross-Culturally*, ed. Filomina Chioma Steady (Cambridge, Mass.: Schenkman Publishing Co., 1981), pp. 79–106.

43. Michelle Z. Rosaldo, "The Use and Abuse of Anthropology: Reflections on Feminism and Cross-Cultural Understanding," *Signs* 5, no. 3 (1980): 389–417.

44. Ibid.

Chapter 2

1. See Christopher Fyfe, "Reform in West Africa: The Abolition of the Slave Trade," in *History of West Africa*, ed. J. F. A. Ajayi and Michael Crowder, vol. 2 (New York: Columbia University Press, 1972); James W. St. G. Walker, *The Black Loyalists: The Search for a Promised Land in Nova Scotia and Sierra Leone, 1783–1870* (New York: Africana Publishing Co.,

1976); and Ellen Gibson Wilson, *The Loyal Blacks* (New York: G. P. Putnam's Sons, 1976).

2. Rhoda Howard, *Colonialism and Underdevelopment in Ghana* (New York: Africana Publishing Co., 1978), p. 29.

3. See Daniel R. Headrick, *The Tools of Empire: Technology and European Imperialism in the Nineteenth Century* (New York: Oxford University Press, 1981).

4. Any history of Sierra Leone that has the black settlers as central figures risks the serious problem of underemphasizing the active role of interior peoples in the Afro-European trade. Although important, the settler's activities should be seen as only one aspect of this nineteenth-century political and economic drama.

5. See T. D. P. Dalby, "Language Distribution in Sierra Leone," *Sierra Leone Language Review* 1 (1962): 62–67.

6. C. Magbaily Fyle, *The Solima Yalunka Kingdom: Pre-Colonial Politics, Economics and Society* (Freetown: Nyakon Publishers, 1979), p. 8.

7. See C. Magbaily Fyle, "Precolonial Commerce in Northeastern Sierra Leone," African Studies Center Working Papers, no. 10 (Boston: Boston University, 1979).

8. See Allen M. Howard, "The Relevance of Spatial Analysis for African Economic History: The Sierra Leone–Guinea System," *Journal of African History* 17 (1976): 365–88; and idem, "Big Men, Traders, and Chiefs: Power, Commerce, and Spatial Change in the Sierra Leone–Guinea Plain, 1865–1895" (Ph.D. diss., University of Wisconsin, 1972).

9. Barbara Harrell-Bond, Allen Howard, and David Skinner, *Community Leadership and Transformation of Freetown (1801–1976)* (The Hague: Mouton Publishers, 1978), p. 22.

10. Ibid.

11. A smaller, economically less important system evolved around Sherbro Island and the nearby rivers that acted as trade routes to its hinterland. Although the region never drew as much attention as the Sierra Leone–Guinea system, in the late nineteenth century it became a center of missionary activity and an important base for Sierra Leone's women traders.

12. Sidney Mintz and Richard Price, *An Anthropological Approach to the Afro-American Past: A Caribbean Perspective* (Philadelphia: Institute for the Study of Human Issues, 1977).

13. Herbert G. Gutman, *The Black Family in Slavery and Freedom, 1750–1925* (New York: Vintage Books, 1977); Eugene D. Genovese, *Roll, Jordan, Roll: The World the Slaves Made* (New York: Pantheon Books, 1974); John W. Blassingame, *The Slave Community: Plantation Life in the Antebellum South* (New York: Oxford University Press, 1972).

14. Robin W. Winks, *The Blacks in Canada: A History* (New Haven: Yale University Press, 1971), p. 41.

15. Christopher Fyfe, *A History of Sierra Leone* (London: Oxford University Press, 1962), p. 102.

16. Ibid., p. 65.

17. Blassingame, *The Slave Community*, p. 17.

18. Walker, *The Black Loyalists*, p. 74.

19. George P. Rawick, *From Sundown to Sunup: The Making of the Black Community* (Westport, Conn.: Greenwood Press, 1972), pp. 30–51.

20. Wilson, *The Loyal Blacks*, p. 113.

21. E. G. Ingham, *Sierra Leone after a Hundred Years* (London: Seely and Co., 1894), p. 136; Walker, *The Black Loyalists*, p. 193.

22. Fyfe, *History of Sierra Leone*, p. 102.

23. Robert Phillip, *The Life, Times and Missionary Enterprises of Rev. Campbell* (London: John Snow, 1841), pp. 175–76; Wilson, *The Loyal Blacks*, p. 13.

24. Fyfe, *History of Sierra Leone*, pp. 101–2.

25. Wilson, *The Loyal Blacks*, p. 355.

26. *Ibid.*, pp. 355–56.

27. Fyfe, *History of Sierra Leone*, p. 102.

28. Wilson, *The Loyal Blacks*, p. 314.

29. PP, vol. 20, 1825, p. 69; Fyfe, *History of Sierra Leone*, p. 143.

30. Elizabeth Melville, *A Residence at Sierra Leone* (London: John Murray, 1849), p. 242.

31. Walker, *The Black Loyalists,* pp. 285–86; Neil Owen Leighton, "Lebanese Middlemen in Sierra Leone: The Case of a Non-Indigenous Trading Minority and Their Role in Political Development" (Ph.D. diss., Indiana University, 1971).

32. Walker, *The Black Loyalists*, pp. 313–14.

33. See, for example, Orlando Patterson, "Slavery and Slave Revolts: A Sociohistorical Analysis of the First Maroon War, Jamaica, 1655–1740," *Social and Economic Studies* 19, no. 3 (September, 1970): 289–325; Mavis C. Campbell, "The Maroons of Jamaica: *Imperium in Imperio?" Pan African Journal* 6, no. 1 (Spring 1973): 45–55; and Roger Bastide, *African Civilization in the New World*, trans. Peter Green (New York: Harper and Row, 1971).

34. For distinctions between settler and nonsettler societies, see Franklin W. Knight, *The African Dimension in Latin American Societies* (New York: Macmillan Co., 1974), pp. 45–46.

35. Mintz and Price, *Anthropological Approach*, pp. 38–42.

36. Robert Charles Dallas, *The History of the Maroons, from Their Origin to the Establishment of Their Chief Tribe at Sierra Leone, etc.*, vol. 1 (London:

Longman and Rees, 1803), p. 198; Barbara K. Kopytoff, "The Maroons of Jamaica: An Ethnohistorical Study of Incomplete Politics" (Ph.D. diss., University of Pennsylvania, 1973), p. 68.

37. B. Kopytoff, "Maroons of Jamaica," p. 68. In contrast, the Windward Maroons who lived on another side of the island killed men and whipped women for committing adultery. Kopytoff attributes these different approaches to differences in the political structure. "The centralization of power and the continuity of chieftaincy gave a stability to Leeward Maroons society that allowed the development of social controls more subtle than those of the Windward Maroons, at least the Maroons of Nanny Town" (p. 305).

38. William J. Gardner, *A History of Jamaica from Its Discovery by Christopher Columbus to the Year 1872* (London, 1872), pp. 225–26.

39. Ibid., p. 238.

40. Dallas, *History of Maroons*, vol. 2, p. 225.

41. J. J. Crooks, *A History of the Colony of Sierra Leone*, (Dublin: Frank Cass, 1903), pp. 57, 76.

42. Fyfe, *History of Sierra Leone*, pp. 101–3.

43. Walker, *The Black Loyalists*, p. 276.

44. The apprenticeship system was designed both to provide for the Liberated Africans without costing the government much money and to integrate the Recaptives into colony life. See Ibid., p. 277.

45. Census of Sierra Leone and Its Dependencies Taken in 1881, CMS G3.A1/L114; Ingham, *Sierra Leone*, pp. 136, 292, 316–17. The Sierra Leone peninsula was characterized by resistant gabbroid rocks and land heavily leached by extremely high rainfall. See R. J. Harrison Church, *West Africa: A Study of the Environment and Man's Use of It* (London: Oxford University Press, 1957), pp. 303–4, 307.

46. PP, vol. 20, 1826, p. 128.

47. Walker, *The Black Loyalists*, pp. 334–35.

48. Ibid., pp. 360–61. He errs also because he looks only at Liberated African elites, those most likely to be noticed by European observers. Many African customs were maintained secretly through organizations such as the hunting societies. Even elites participated in these organizations, but they did not share these experiences with Europeans.

49. See J. F. A. Ajayi, "The Aftermath of the Fall of Old Oyo," in *History of West Africa*, ed. J. F. A. Ajayi and Michael Crowder, vol. 2 (London: Longman Press, 1974), pp. 129–66; and J. F. A. Ajayi and Robert Smith, *Yoruba Warfare in the Nineteenth Century* (Cambridge: Cambridge University Press, 1971).

50. John Peterson, "Independence and Innovations in the Nineteenth Century Colony Village," *Sierra Leone Studies*, n.s., 21 (July, 1967): 3;

Robert Clarke, *Sierra Leone: A Description of the Manners and Customs of the Liberated African* (London: James Ridgeway and Co., 1843), p. 23. The origin of the term *Aku* is in dispute. John Peterson suggests that the name stemmed from a Yoruba greeting, *akuseio. Province of Freedom: A History of Sierra Leone, 1787–1870* (London: Faber and Faber, 1969), p. 324 n. 41. Gibril R. Cole argues that Peterson is wrong and cites oral traditions in the Aku Muslim community to support his contention that it is derived from the Yoruba word for dead, *oku.* "Krio Muslim Society of Freetown: A Case Study of Fourah Bay and Fourah Town, 1810–1910" (B.A. honors thesis, Fourah Bay College, 1978), pp. 68–69.

51. Harrell-Bond, Howard, and Skinner, *Community Leadership,* pp. 121–25.

52. Clarke, *Sierra Leone,* p. 40.

53. Quoted in N. A. Cox-George, *Finance and Development in West Africa: The Sierra Leone Experience* (London: Denis Dobson, 1961), p. 149.

54. James Africanus Beale Horton, *West African Countries and Peoples* (1868; reprint, Edinburgh: Edinburgh University Press, 1969), p. 140.

55. I. A. Akinjogbin, "The Expansion of Oyo and the Rise of Dahomey, 1600–1800," in *History of West Africa,* ed. J. F. A. Ajayi and Michael Crowder, vol. 1 (London: Longman Press, 1971), p. 311; Robin Law, *The Oyo Empire, c. 1600–c. 1836: A West African Imperialism in the Era of the Atlantic Slave Trade* (Oxford: Clarendon Press, 1977), p. 216.

56. Samuel Johnson, *The History of the Yorubas from the Earliest Times to the Beginning of the British Protectorate* (London: Church Missionary Society, 1921), p. 218.

57. Ibid., pp. 207–8.

58. Ibid., p. 118.

59. Daryll Forde, *The Yoruba-Speaking Peoples of South-Western Nigeria* (London: International African Institute, 1962), p. 8; Law, *The Oyo Empire,* p. 210.

60. Samuel O. Biobaku, *The Egba and Their Neighbors, 1842–1872* (Oxford: Clarendon Press, 1971), p. 6.

61. Simi Afonja, "Changing Modes of Production and the Sexual Division of Labor among the Yoruba," *Signs* 7, no. 2 (Winter 1981): 311.

62. Ibid.

63. Quoted in Babatunde Agiri, "Slavery in Yoruba Society in the Nineteenth Century," in *The Ideology of Slavery in Africa,* ed. Paul E. Lovejoy (Beverly Hills: Sage Publications, 1980), p. 35.

64. Ibid., p. 134.

65. Afonja, "Changing Modes of Production," pp. 308–9.

66. Law, *The Oyo Empire,* p. 231.

67. Hugh Clapperton, *Journal of a Second Expedition into the Interior of*

Africa from the Bight of Benin to Soccatto (1829; reprint, London: Frank Cass and Co., 1966), p. 6.

68. Johnson, *History of the Yorubas*, p. 63.

69. Ibid., p. 77.

70. Paul E. Lovejoy, "Slavery in the Context of Ideology," in *The Ideology of Slavery in Africa*, ed. Paul E. Lovejoy (Beverly Hills: Sage Publications, 1980), pp. 11–38.

71. Niara Sudarkasa, "Female Employment and Family Organization in West Africa," in *The Black Woman Cross-Culturally*, ed. Filomina Chioma Steady (Cambridge, Mass.: Schenkman Publishing Co., 1981), p. 53.

72. Lovejoy, "Slavery in the Context of Ideology," p. 21.

73. Paul E. Lovejoy, *Transformations in Slavery: A History of Slavery in Africa* (Cambridge: Cambridge University Press, 1983), p. 92; Svend E. Holsoe, "Slavery and Economic Response among the Vai (Liberia and Sierra Leone)," in *Slavery in Africa: Historical and Anthropological Perspectives*, ed. Suzanne Miers and Igor Kopytoff (Madison: University of Wisconsin Press, 1977), p. 290.

74. Adam Jones, *From Slaves to Palm Kernels: A History of the Galinhas Country (West Africa), 1730–1890* (Wiesbaden: Steiner, 1983), p. 190; Claire Robertson and Martin A. Klein, "Women's Importance in African Slave Systems," in *Women and Slavery in Africa*, ed. Claire Robertson and Martin A. Klein (Madison: University of Wisconsin Press, 1983), p. 10.

75. Carol P. MacCormack, "Wono: Institutionalized Dependency in Sherbro Descent Groups," in *Slavery in Africa*, ed. Suzanne Miers and Igor Kopytoff (Madison: University of Wisconsin Press, 1977), p. 188.

76. Ibid.

77. David E. Skinner, *Thomas George Lawson: African Historian and Administrator in Sierra Leone* (Stanford: Hoover Institution Press, 1980), p. 60.

78. Lovejoy, *Transformations in Slavery*, pp. 162–63.

79. Ibid., p. 163; Skinner, *Thomas George Lawson*, p. 59; MacCormack, "Wono," p. 192.

80. Quoted in Crooks, *History of the Colony*, pp. 174–75.

81. Quoted in ibid., pp. 131–32.

82. C. B. Jones to H. E. Harper, December 20, 1836, Liberated African Letter Book, Sierra Leone Government Archives.

83. Fyfe, *History of Sierra Leone*, p. 192.

84. Ester Boserup, *Woman's Role in Economic Development* (New York: St. Martin's Press, 1970), pp. 37–52. This is not to argue that only economic reasons influenced the development of polygynous marriage practices.

85. Johnson, *History of the Yorubas*, p. 116.

86. Reade, *African Sketch-Book*, pp. 388–89; emphasis in original.

87. Fyfe, *History of Sierra Leone*, p. 192.

88. The 1831 census identified several female-headed households in which women appeared to be the main economic support. Ibid., p. 192.

89. *Sierra Leone Weekly News* (hereafter cited as *SLWN*), May 13, 1905. Fufu and gari are both made from cassava.

90. Clarke, *Sierra Leone*, p. 27.

91. Ibid., p. 7.

92. Ibid., pp. 35–36.

93. PP, vol. 20, 1826, p. 128.

94. F. Harrison Rankin, *The White Man's Grave: A Visit to Sierra Leone in 1834* (London: Richard Bentley, 1836), vol. 1, p. 223.

95. A. B. C. Sibthorpe, *The History of Sierra Leone* (London: Elliot Stock, 1881), p. 56.

96. Mary Church, *Liberated Africans, In a Series of Letters from a Young Lady to her Sister in 1833 and 1834* (London: Longman and Co., 1835), p. 46.

97. Fyfe, *History of Sierra Leone*, pp. 204–5.

98. Ibid., pp. 211–12.

99. Ibid., pp. 257, 471.

100. F. W. Butt-Thompson, *Sierra Leone in History and Tradition* (London: H. F. and G. W. Witherby, 1926), p. 50.

101. Fyfe, *History of Sierra Leone*, pp. 333, 366.

102. Ibid., p. 437.

103. Ibid., p. 536; Butt-Thompson, *Sierra Leone in History*, p. 50.

104. I. C. Hotobah-During, interview with author, January 1, 1981; O. Willis Benjamins, interview with author, January 15, 1981.

105. Governor MacDonald to Secretary of State, Dispatch 132, October, 1850, Public Record Office (hereafter cited as PRO): Colonial Office (hereafter cited as CO) 267/216.

106. H. Osman Newland, *Sierra Leone: Its People, Products, and Secret Societies* (London: John Bale and Sons and Danielson, 1916), p. 17.

107. Governor Hill to Secretary of State, Dispatch 146, June 29, 1861, PRO: CO 267/299. Among the myths that have grown up around the Big Market is the belief that the Portuguese built the marketplace. Judy Vincent, interview with author, October 9, 1976; Abigail Coker-Black, interview with author, March 2, 1976.

108. Governor Hill to Secretary of State, Dispatch 148, June 29, 1861, PRO: CO 267/112.

109. Theodore Jones, interview with author, September 30, 1976.

110. Richard Burton, *Wanderings in West Africa: From Liverpool to Fernando Po*, vol. 1 (London: Tinsley Brothers, 1863), pp. 228–30.

111. Ibid., pp. 230–31.

112. G. A. L. Banbury, *Sierra Leone or the White Man's Grave* (London: S. Sonnenshein, 1888), pp. 146–47.

113. Allen Howard, "Historical Centralities and Spatial Patterns in Northern Sierra Leone" (Paper presented at the Joint Committee on African Studies of the American Council of Learned Societies/Social Science Research Council Conference on Spatial Hierarchies in African Interurban Systems, New York, 1970); see Walter Christaller, *Central Places in Southern Germany*, trans. Carlisle W. Baskin (Englewood Cliffs, N.J.: Prentice Hall, 1966); A. Losch, *The Economics of Location*, trans. W. H. Woylon (New Haven: Yale University Press, 1954), p. 31.

114. Robert J. Olu-Wright, "The Physical Growth of Freetown," in *Freetown: A Symposium*, ed. Christopher Fyfe and Eldred Jones (Freetown: University of Sierra Leone Press, 1968), p. 31.

115. T. Jones, interview with author, September 30, 1976; Hotobah-During, interview with author, May 27, 1976.

116. Josephine Slowe, interview with author, September 19, 1976.

117. Mary Williams, interview with author, November 10, 1976; Sarian During, interview with author, December 29, 1976.

118. Edna Decker, interview with author, November 10, 1976.

119. Cf. Daniel F. McCall, "The Koforidua Market," in *Markets in Africa*, ed. Paul Bohannon and George Dalton (Evanston: Northwestern University Press, 1962), pp. 667–97.

120. Princess James, interview with author, October 15, 1976; Hotobah-During, interview with author, May 29, 1976. Among the Yoruba, this special customer relationship was called *onibara*. See Lillian Trager, "Customers and Credit: Variations in Economic Personalisms in a Nigerian Market System," *Ethnology* 20, no. 2 (April, 1981): 133–46.

121. T. Jones, interview with author, December 6, 1976.

122. Farian Coker, interview with author, December 18, 1975.

123. Ibid.; Vincent, interview with author, October 9, 1976.

124. Leo Spitzer, *The Creoles of Sierra Leone: Responses to Colonialism, 1870–1949* (Madison: University of Wisconsin Press, 1974); Arthur T. Porter, *Creoledom: A Study of the Development of Freetown Society* (Oxford: Oxford University Press, 1963); Fyfe, *History of Sierra Leone*.

125. Christopher Fyfe, "European and Creole Influences in the Hinterland of Sierra Leone Before 1896," *Sierra Leone Studies*, n.s., no. 6 (1956), p. 116; Horton, *West African Countries and Peoples*, p. 140.

126. Allen Howard, "Kola Production and Trade in Sierra Leone, 1850–1930" (Paper presented at the University of London School of Oriental and African Studies and Institute of Commonwealth Studies, London, May 16, 1979), p. 2.

127. Ibid. See also George E. Brooks, Jr., "Kola Trade and State-Building: Upper Guinea Coast and Senegambia, 15th to 17th Centuries," African Studies Center Working Papers, no. 38 (Boston: Boston University, 1980).

128. Paul E. Lovejoy, "The Hausa Kola Trade (1700–1900): A Commercial System in the Continental Exchange of West Africa" (Ph.D. diss., University of Wisconsin, 1973), p. 5.

129. Stephen B. Baier, "African Merchants in the Colonial Period: A History of Commerce in Damagaram (Central Niger), 1880–1960 (Ph.D. diss., University of Wisconsin, 1974), p. 148. In 1815, Liberated Africans withdrew from one of the British-created villages, Hastings, to establish their own village, Abeokola. The Yoruba-sounding name derives from the main commercial function of the town and indicates an early participation in the kola trade. Peterson, *Province of Freedom*, pp. 206–7.

130. Howard, "Kola Production," pp. 5–6.

131. Thomas Joshua Alldridge, *The Sherbro and Its Hinterland* (London: Macmillan and Co., 1901), p. 41.

132. Lovejoy, "The Hausa Kola Trade," p. 195; Baier, "African Merchants," pp. 149–50. Saro is a corruption of the words "Sierra Leone."

133. Babatunde Agiri, "The Introduction of Nitida Kola into Nigerian Agriculture, 1880–1920," *African Economic History* 3 (Spring 1977): 5–6.

134. See, for example, Sierra Leone Trade Reports, Native Affairs Minute Papers (hereafter cited as NAMP) no. 193, 1897; no. 316, 1897; no. 347, 1898; and no. 349, 1898, Sierra Leone Government Archives.

135. John Davidson, "Trade and Politics in the Sherbro Hinterland, 1849–1890" (Ph.D. diss., University of Wisconsin, 1969), pp. 79–80.

136. Ibid., pp. 91–93.

137. Ibid., p. 129.

138. Alldridge, *The Sherbro*, p. 41.

139. Lillie Mae Domingo, interview with author, January 22, 1977; *Annual Report for Sierra Leone, 1902* (Freetown: Sierra Leone Government), p. 14.

140. Alldridge, *The Sherbro*, p. 73; *SLWN*, November 5, 1904.

141. *Annual Report for Sierra Leone, 1899* (Freetown, Sierra Leone Government), p. 25.

142. Cole, "Krio Muslim Society," pp. 89–90; Laura Hero Cline, interview with author, January 22, 1981; P. Allizas Robinson, interview with author, January 14, 1981.

143. Florence K. Omolara Mahoney, "Government and Opinion in The Gambia, 1816–1901" (Ph.D. diss., London University, 1963), pp. 138–39.

144. Ibid., p. 139.

145. Philip D. Curtin, *Economic Change in Precolonial Africa: Senegambia in the Era of the Slave Trade* (Madison: University of Wisconsin Press, 1975), pp. 60, 229, 295.

146. Abner Cohen, "Cultural Strategies in the Organization of Trading Diasporas," in *The Development of Indigenous Trade and Markets in West Africa*, ed. Claude Meillassoux and Daryll Forde (London: Oxford University Press, 1971), pp. 271–76.

147. Alldridge, *The Sherbro*, p. 41.

148. Curtin, *Economic Change*, p. 295.

149. E.g., Spitzer, *Creoles of Sierra Leone;* Porter, *Creoledom;* and Hargraves, *Life of Sir Samuel Lewis.* See chapter 1 above for a critique of this view.

150. Domingo, interview with author, January 22, 1977.

151. Peterson, *Province of Freedom*, p. 250.

152. Ibid., pp. 250–51.

153. Ibid., p. 268.

154. Cole, "Krio Muslim Society," pp. 73–74.

155. *SLWN*, January 29, 1887; February 5, 1887; February 19, 1887; February 26, 1887; May 12, 1888. See also Akintola J. G. Wyse, "Sierra Leone Creoles: Their History and Historians," *Journal of African Studies* 4, no. 2 (Summer 1977): 228–39.

156. Carol P. Hoffer, "Mende and Sherbro Women in High Office," *Canadian Journal of African Studies* 6, no. 2 (1972): 162.

157. Priscilla Hinckley, "The Sowo Mask: Symbol of Sisterhood," African Studies Center Working Papers, no. 40 (Boston: Boston University, 1980); Carol P. Hoffer, "Bundu: Political Implications of Female Solidarity in a Secret Society," in *Being Female: Reproduction, Power, and Change* (The Hague: Mouton Publishers, 1975), p. 160.

158. Hinckley, "The Sowo Mask," p. 4.

159. Cf. Judith Van Allen, "'Aba Riots' or Igbo 'Women's War'? Ideology, Stratification, and the Invisibility of Women," in *Women in Africa: Studies in Social and Economic Change*, ed. Nancy Hafkin and Edna Bay (Stanford: Stanford University Press, 1976).

160. Hoffer, "Mende and Sherbro Women," p. 160; Oji Anya, "The Sherbro in the Nineteenth Century: A Coastal People in Transition" (Master's thesis, Fourah Bay College, 1973), pp. 19–22.

161. Anya, "The Sherbro in the Nineteenth Century," p. 10.

162. Janet M. Bujra, "Introductory: Female Solidarity and the Sexual Division of Labour," in *Women United, Women Divided*, ed. Patricia Caplan and Janet M. Bujra (London: Travistock Publications, 1978), p. 33. Cf. Caroline Bledsoe, *Women and Marriage in Kpelle Society* (Stanford: Stanford University Press, 1980).

163. For a critique of this view see Gustav K. Deveneux, "The Political and Social Impact of the Colony in Northern Sierra Leone, 1821–1896" (Ph.D. diss., Boston University, 1973), pp. 382–90.

164. Sierra Leone Trade at Kambia, September, 1895, NAMP no. 527; Sierra Leone Trade at Kambia, October, 1895, NAMP no. 597.

165. Robbery Committed in Her Store at Kambia, J. C. Ernest Parkes to Alikarli Koya Bubu, October 27, 1894, Native Affairs Letter Book (hereafter cited as NALB) no. 474, Sierra Leone Government Archives.

166. Mrs. Wilson's Complaint against the Alikarli of Kambia, J. C. Ernest Parkes to Bey Farima, January 2, 1895, NALB no. 5.

167. See the important work by V. R. Dorjahn and Christopher Fyfe, "Landlord and Stranger: Change in Tenancy Relations in Sierra Leone," *Journal of African History* 3, no. 3 (1962): 391–97; that first examined the position of Sierra Leone strangers in the interior.

168. Georg Simmel, "The Stranger," in *The Sociology of Georg Simmel,* trans. and ed. Kurt H. Wolf (New York: Free Press, 1950), p. 145; Donald N. Levine, "Simmel at a Distance: On the History and Systematics of the Sociology of the Stranger," in *Strangers in African Societies,* ed. William A. Shack and Elliot P. Skinner (Berkeley: University of California Press, 1979), pp. 21–36.

169. William A. Shack, "Introduction," in *Strangers in African Societies,* ed. William A. Shack and Elliot P. Skinner (Berkeley: University of California Press, 1979), p. 15.

170. See, for example, Neil Owen Leighton, "The Political Economy of a Stranger Population: The Lebanese of Sierra Leone"; and Hershelle Sullivan Challenor, "Strangers as Colonial Intermediaries: The Dahomeyans in Francophone, Africa," both in *Strangers in African Societies,* ed. William A. Shack and Elliot P. Skinner (Berkeley: University of California Press, 1979), pp. 67–103.

171. Shack, "Introduction," pp. 10–11.

172. Davidson, "Trade and Politics," pp. 147–48.

173. Sarah Faux [Fox] to Governor, August 14, 1869, Local Letters to the Governor (hereafter cited as LLG), Sierra Leone Government Archives.

174. Thomas G. Lawson to Acting Colonial Secretary, August 17, 1869, LLG.

175. A similar argument could be made about Muslim or Christian missionaries.

176. Elliot P. Skinner, "Conclusions," in *Strangers in African Societies,* ed. William A. Shack and Elliot P. Skinner (Berkeley: University of California Press, 1979), p. 281.

177. Reade, *African Sketch-Book,* pp. 398–40; Jones, *From Slaves to Palm Kernels,* p. 154.

178. Sierra Leone Legislative Council Debates, 1925–26 (Freetown: Sierra Leone Government), p. 20.

179. Anthony G. Hopkins, *An Economic History of West Africa* (New York: Columbia University Press, 1973), p. 113.

180. Leighton, "Lebanese Middlemen," p. 81.

181. Ibid., pp. 81–82.

182. Cox-George, *Finance and Development*, pp. 69–70; see especially Spitzer, *Creoles of Sierra Leone*, pp. 56–58.

183. Cox-George, *Finance and Development*, pp. 69–70.

184. Michael Crowder, *West Africa Under Colonial Rule* (London: Hutchinson and Co., 1968), pp. 184–85. See also Michael Crowder and LaRay Denzer, "Bai Bureh and the Sierra Leone Hut Tax War of 1898," in *Protest and Power in Black Africa*, ed. Robert I. Rotberg and Ali Mazrui (London: Oxford University Press, 1970), pp. 160–212.

185. Chalmers Report, PP, vol. 60, 1899, p. 145.

186. Ibid., p. 234.

Chapter 3

1. Leo Spitzer, *The Creoles of Sierra Leone: Responses to Colonialism, 1870–1949* (Madison: University of Wisconsin Press, 1974), p. 157.

2. Michael Crowder, *West Africa Under Colonial Rule* (London: Hutchinson and Co., 1968), p. 254.

3. Ibid., p. 268 n. 29.

4. Ibid., p. 257.

5. Ruth Hollis, interview with author, November 30, 1976.

6. Mary Williams, interview with author, December 19, 1976.

7. Crowder, *West Africa*, p. 257.

8. Ibid., p. 258.

9. N. A. Cox-George, *Finance and Development in West Africa: The Sierra Leone Experience* (London: Denis Dobson, 1961), p. 173.

10. Crowder, *West Africa*, p. 256.

11. Cox-George, *Finance and Development*, p. 299.

12. Ibid., pp. 163–64; Crowder, *West Africa*, p. 299. See also P. N. Davies, *The Trade Makers: Elder Dempster in West Africa, 1852–1972* (London: Allen and Unwin, 1973).

13. Cox-George, *Finance and Development*, p. 299.

14. Cf. Allen Howard, "The Role of Freetown in the Commercial Life of Sierra Leone," in *Freetown: A Symposium*, ed. Christopher Fyfe and Eldred Jones (Freetown: University of Sierra Leone Press, 1966), p. 48. Anthony Hopkins, however, has argued that the decline of Africans in the import/export firms should not be exaggerated because European firms had already begun to dominate the trade of the coastal ports during the 1850–80 period. In addition, the value of African-controlled external

trade was greater in the 1920s than in the previous century. Hopkins notes that "what happened was that all groups gained from the expansion of trade during the first phase of colonial rule, but the expatriate firms gained relatively more than the indigenous firms." *An Economic History of West Africa* (New York: Columbia University Press, 1973), p. 204.

15. Hopkins, *Economic History*, p. 202.

16. Crowder, *West Africa*, p. 299; Hopkins, *Economic History*, p. 202.

17. Rhoda Howard, *Colonialism and Underdevelopment in Ghana* (New York: Africana Publishing Co., 1978), p. 185.

18. Hopkins, *Economic History*, p. 256.

19. Crowder, *West Africa*, pp. 258–59.

20. Spitzer, *Creoles of Sierra Leone*, pp. 151–70 passim.

21. Cox-George, *Finance and Development*, pp. 162–63.

22. R. Bayly Winder, "The Lebanese in West Africa," *Comparative Studies in Sociology and History* 4 (1962): 297–98. See also Marwan Hanna, "The Lebanese in West Africa," *West Africa*, no. 2142 (May 3, 1958): 415.

23. Neil Owen Leighton, "The Political Economy of a Stranger Population: The Lebanese of Sierra Leone," in *Strangers in African Societies*, ed. William A. Shack and Elliot P. Skinner (Berkeley: University of California Press, 1979), p. 88.

24. Winder, "Lebanese in West Africa," p. 309; Hopkins, *Economic History*, p. 206.

25. Neil Owen Leighton, "Lebanese Middlemen in Sierra Leone: The Case of a Non-Indigenous Trading Minority and Their Role in Political Development" (Ph.D. diss., Indiana University, 1971), p. 40.

26. Leighton, "Political Economy of a Stranger Population," p. 86.

27. In fact, the much-feared alliance did eventually occur. Ibid., p. 99.

28. Leighton, "Lebanese Middlemen in Sierra Leone," pp. 192–93. Cf. R. Howard, *Colonialism and Underdevelopment*, pp. 18–19.

29. Leighton, "Lebanese Middlemen in Sierra Leone," p. 192.

30. Arthur T. Porter, *Creoledom: A Study of the Development of Freetown Society* (Oxford: Oxford University Press, 1963), p. 113.

31. Ibid., p. 127.

32. Abner Cohen, "The Politics of Ritual Secrecy," *Man* 6 (1971): 429; idem, *The Politics of Elite Culture: Explorations in the Dramaturgy of Power in a Modern African Society* (Berkeley: University of California Press, 1981), pp. xviii–xix.

33. I. C. Hotobah-During, interview with author, June 6, 1976.

34. James W. St. G. Walker, *The Black Loyalists: The Search for a Promised Land in Nova Scotia and Sierra Leone, 1783–1870* (New York: Africana Publishing Co., 1976), pp. 334–35; John Peterson, *Province of Freedom: A History of Sierra Leone, 1787–1870* (London: Faber and Faber, 1969), p.

204; Christopher Fyfe, *A History of Sierra Leone* (London: Oxford University Press, 1962), pp. 269–70.

35. Cf. William G. Davis, *Social Relations in a Philippine Market: Self-Interest and Subjectivity* (Berkeley: University of California Press, 1973), for a discussion of the success of the Chinese minority in the Philippines and the role of kinship organization in this success. On the one hand, the lowland Filipinos he studied reckoned descent bilaterally, and thus lacked a strong kinship reference point. On the other hand, the Chinese focused on males and emphasized the principle of patrilineal descent. This principle fostered corporate kinship forms and collective economic behavior. While the lowland Filipinos did develop kinship firms, they were rarely as strong as those of the Chinese (pp. 197–99).

See also Alice G. Dewey, *Peasant Marketing in Java* (Glencoe, Ill.: Free Press, 1962) who also asserted the importance of kinship ties in Chinese commercial successes in Indonesia. In addition, she mentions in a footnote that in the colonial era the Dutch suppressed the Javanese but favored the Chinese as intermediaries, "as they were few in number and more easily controlled" (pp. 46–47).

36. H. L. van der Laan, *The Lebanese Traders in Sierra Leone* (The Hague: Mouton Publishers, 1976), pp. 228–29. The Lebanese family firms did have disadvantages, however. For example, "the family enterprise has not been a good school for delegating tasks, for even grown-up sons received little freedom of action if they were in charge of a separate shop" (p. 229).

37. Porter, *Creoledom*, p. 114; Joko H. M. Smart, "Inheritance to Property in Sierra Leone: An Analysis of the Law and Problems Involved," *Sierra Leone Studies*, n.s., no. 24 (January, 1969): 6–7.

38. SLWN, March 7, 1885.

39. Hotobah-During, interview with author, January 7, 1981; Beatrice Victoria Short, interview with author, January 15, 1981; Vivi Johnson, interview with author, January 6, 1981.

40. Four women, three in their eighties and one just turning sixty, used this saying to describe the struggle between themselves and their husbands when they first married. Short, interview with author, January 15, 1981; Princess James, interview with author, November 2, 1976; Mary Beckles, interview with author, September 28, 1976; Judy Vincent, interview with author, October 9, 1976.

41. Short, interview with author, January 15, 1981; Beckles, interview with author, September 28, 1976; Abigail Coker-Black, interview with author, March 3, 1976.

42. *Annual Report for Sierra Leone, 1901* (Freetown: Sierra Leone Government).

43. *Annual Report for Sierra Leone, 1910* (Freetown: Sierra Leone Government).

44. Ibid.

45. *Annual Report for Sierra Leone, 1913; Annual Report for Sierra Leone, 1915* (Freetown: Sierra Leone Government).

46. *Annual Report, 1913.*

47. Lucy Tucker, interview with author, January 21, 1977.

48. Vincent, interview with author, December 10, 1976; Sarah Scott, interview with author, January 11, 1981.

49. Onika Clarrisa Bull, interview with author, January 5, 1981; V. Johnson, interview with author, January 16, 1981.

50. Allen Howard, "Kola Production and Trade in Sierra Leone, 1850–1930" (Paper presented at the University of London School of Oriental and African Studies and Institute of Commonwealth Studies, London, May 16, 1979), pp. 9–10. In addition, the sudden decline of Guinea-Bissau as an importer affected the Krios' hold on the trade as they had also been well placed in Bissau.

51. Van der Laan, *Lebanese Traders*, p. 78.

52. *SLWN*, June 12, 1919; June 28, 1919; July 12, 1919; Spitzer, *Creoles of Sierra Leone*, pp. 159–60.

53. Spitzer, *Creoles of Sierra Leone*, p. 160.

54. Ibid., p. 163.

55. Ibid., pp. 166–67; Martin H. Y. Kaniki, "Attitudes and Reactions towards the Lebanese in Sierra Leone during the Colonial Period," *Canadian Journal of African Studies* 8, no. 1 (1973): 97.

56. Evelyn to Milner, September 4, 1919, PRO, CO 267/582.

57. *SLWN*, August 19, 1919.

58. *SLWN*, September 6, 1919.

59. *SLWN*, June 12, 1920.

60. Spitzer, *Creoles of Sierra Leone*, pp. 167–74.

61. Theodore Jones, interview with author, February 10, 1976; Hotobah-During, interview with author, May 17, 1976; Sarian During, interview with author, December 19, 1976; Miranda Coker, interview with author, January 22, 1977; Ruth C. Wright, interview with author, January 5, 1981; Lucinda O. Jones, interview with author, January 5, 1981. Some Krio women, especially Muslim women of Foulah Town and Fourah Bay, are still involved in the kola trade with Senegambia, but their portion of the trade is much smaller than it was in the late nineteenth and early twentieth centuries.

62. S. During, interview with author, December 20, 1976.

63. T. Jones, interview with author, June 20, 1976; Hotobah-During, interview with author, May 19, 1976; Vincent, interview with author, October 6, 1976; Coker-Black, interview with author, March 3, 1976.

64. Crowder, *West Africa*, p. 257.

65. Vincent, interview with author, October 9, 1976.

66. *West Africa*, July 30, 1919.

67. Vincent, interview with author, October 17, 1976.

68. Vincent, interview with author, October 9, 1976.

69. LaRay Denzer, personal communication with author, December 27, 1976. See also LaRay Denzer and Leo Spitzer, "I. T. A. Wallace-Johnson and the West African Youth League," *International Journal of African Historical Studies* 6, nos. 3–4 (1973): 413–52, 565–601.

70. Hotobah-During, interview with author, May 8, 1976; T. Jones, interview with author, November 11, 1976; Coker-Black, interview with author, November 30, 1976.

71. T. Jones, interview with author, September 30, 1976.

72. T. Jones and Vincent, interviews with author, October 10, 1976.

73. *Daily Mail*, December 16, 1954.

74. Mariana Nyula, interview with author, October 13, 1976; Hotobah-During, interview with author, May 19, 1976. On the move of the Freetown harbor see K. G. Dalton, *A Geography of Sierra Leone* (Cambridge: Cambridge University Press, 1965), p. 19.

75. Sally Davis, interview with author, January 21, 1977; Peter Williams, interview with author, January 21, 1977.

76. M. Coker, interview with author, January 22, 1977.

77. Lillie Mae Domingo, interview with author, January 22, 1977; John Bamiba, interview with author, January 21, 1977.

78. Bamiba, interview with author, January 21, 1977; Tucker, interview with author, January 18, 1977.

79. Cf. Milton Harvey, "Bonthe: A Geographical Study of a Moribund Port and Its Environs," *Bulletin of the Journal of the Sierra Leone Association* 10 (1966): 60–75.

80. George Smith, interview with author, November 10, 1976.

81. Smith, interview with author, December 22, 1976.

82. Beckles, interview with author, September 28, 1976.

83. P. James, interview with author, October 10, 1976.

84. P. James, interview with author, October 15, 1976.

85. Ibid.

86. P. James, interview with author, November 2, 1976.

87. P. James, interview with author, November 3, 1976.

88. Ibid.

89. Ibid.; Tunde James, interview with author, October 4, 1976.

90. P. James, interview with author, November 3, 1976.

91. Hotobah-During, interview with author, October 30, 1976.

92. P. James, interview with author, November 10, 1976.

93. Ibid.; Hotobah-During, interview with author, January 17, 1981.

94. van der Laan, *Lebanese Traders,* p. 169.

95. P. James, interview with author, November 12, 1976; T. James, interviews with author, October 4, 1976 and September 12, 1983.

96. *We Yonne,* January 14, 1981.

97. J. B. Webster, "Political Activity in British West Africa, 1900–1940," in *History of West Africa,* ed. J. F. A. Ajayi and Michael Crowder, vol. 2 (London: Longman Press, 1974), pp. 575–80; Crowder, *West Africa,* pp. 405–71; Spitzer, *Creoles of Sierra Leone,* pp. 171–79; *SLWN,* June 12, 1920.

98. Barbara Harrell-Bond, Allen Howard, and David Skinner, *Community Leadership and the Transformation of Freetown (1801–1976)* (The Hague: Mouton Publishers, 1978), pp. 41–84.

99. Webster, "Political Activity in British West Africa," p. 579.

100. Ibid.

101. Ibid.

102. Spitzer, *Creoles of Sierra Leone,* p. 181.

103. *West Africa,* December 17, 1938.

104. Constance Cummings-John, interview with author, October 3, 1976. See Kwame Nkrumah, *Ghana: An Autobiography* (Edinburgh: Thomas Nelson, 1959).

105. *West Africa,* April 16, 1938.

106. Spitzer, *Creoles of Sierra Leone,* p. 212.

107. LaRay Denzer, personal communication with author, March 4, 1978. The Sierra Leone Marketwomen's Union was a precursor of the Sierra Leone Women's Movement, founded in 1951. The youth league had a position on its central committee for a marketwomen's organizer.

108. Spitzer, *Creoles of Sierra Leone,* p. 215.

109. Cummings-John, interview with author, October 3, 1976; Denzer, personal communcation with author, April 6, 1978.

Chapter 4

1. Adelaide Cromwell Gulliver has focused attention on the value of such biographies to the study of African women. "A Biographical Approach to the Study of African Women in Twentieth Century Socio-Economic Change," (Paper presented at the UCLA African Studies Center Colloquium on Women and Change in Africa, 1870–1970, Los Angeles, April, 1974). For a useful biography, see Felicia Ekejiuba, "Omu Okwesi, the Merchant Queen of Ossomari: A Biographical Sketch," *Journal of the Historical Society of Nigeria* 3, no. 4 (1974): 633–46.

2. Bure Palmer, interview with author, December 29, 1976. Similarly, Omu Okwesi was apprenticed to her maternal aunt in Igala country, where she learned to speak Igala, an important trade language. Ekejiuba, "Omu Okwesi," p. 635.

3. B. Palmer, interview with author, December 29, 1976.

4. See Claire Robertson, "Economic Woman in Africa: Profit-Making Techniques of Accra Market Women," *Journal of Modern African Studies* 12, no. 4 (1967), for a discussion of the use of apprenticeships by women in Accra markets. She maintained that the apprenticeship system offset the disadvantages of illiteracy.

5. B. Palmer, interview with author, January 2, 1976.

6. Ibid.

7. B. Palmer, interview with author, December 28, 1976.

8. Ibid.

9. B. Palmer, interview with author, January 2, 1976.

10. Similar arguments have frequently been made about the role of Islam in the lives of Muslim traders. Cf. Abner Cohen, *Custom and Politics in Urban Africa: A Study of Hausa Migrants in Yoruba Towns* (Berkeley: University of California Press, 1969).

11. Cf. Eleanor Johnson, "Marketwomen and Capitalist Adaptation: A Case Study of Rural Benin, Nigeria," (Ph.D. diss., Michigan State University, 1974), p. 182.

12. See chapter 3 above for a discussion of the Lebanese-Krio competition and the advantages that the former held over the latter.

13. N. A. Cox-George, "Report on African Participation in the Commerce of Sierra Leone and the Government Statement Thereon" (Freetown: Sierra Leone Government 1960), p. 56; Arthur Porter, *Creoledom: A Study of the Development of Freetown Society* (Oxford: Oxford University Press, 1963), pp. 113–14.

14. B. Palmer, interview with author, January 3, 1976.

15. Daniel K. Flickinger, *Ethiopia Coming to God: Missionary Life in West Africa* (Dayton: United Brethren Printing Establishment, 1877); idem, *The History of the Origin, Development and Condition of Missions Among the Sherbro and Mendi Tribes in Western Africa* (Dayton: United Brethren Printing Establishment, 1880); idem, *Off Hand Sketches of Men and Things in Western Africa* (Dayton: United Brethren Printing Establishment, 1887).

16. Lillie Mae Domingo, interview with author, January 22, 1977.

17. Christopher Fyfe, *A History of Sierra Leone* (London: Oxford University Press, 1962), pp. 420–21.

18. Ibid., p. 421.

19. Ibid., p. 473.

20. John Davidson, "Trade and Politics in the Sherbro Hinterland, 1849–1890" (Ph.D. diss., University of Wisconsin, 1969), p. 223. Later, in 1906, Wilberforce was tried for and acquitted of cannibalism. His own explanation for his troubles was that his enemies manufactured a complaint to embarrass him, as he had accepted the Imperi chieftaincy to uproot such practices. *SLWN*, April 28, 1906; May 4, 1906; May 12, 1906.

On his trials and acquittals, see the *Colonial and Provincial Reporter*, April 26, 1913, and May 3, 1913.

21. B. W. Fitch-Jones, "Extracts from a Diary Written During the 1898 Rebellion," *Sierra Leone Studies*, o.s., 17 (February, 1932).

22. Fyfe, *History of Sierra Leone*, p. 572. Oji Anya, "The Sherbro in the Nineteenth Century: A Coastal People in Transition" (Master's thesis, Fourah Bay College, 1973), pp. 46, 54.

23. Domingo, interview with author, January 22, 1977.

24. Domingo, interview with author, January 23, 1977.

25. Domingo, interview with author, January 22, 1977.

26. Domingo, interview with author, January 22, 1977.

27. Davidson, "Trade and Politics," p. 79. See also Kenneth Little, "The Changing Position of Women in the Sierra Leone Protectorate," *Africa* 18, no. 4 (1948): 1–17.

28. Domingo, interview with author, January 22, 1977.

29. See Filomina Chioma Steady, "Protestant Women's Associations in Freetown, Sierra Leone," in *Women in Africa: Studies in Social and Economic Change*, ed. Nancy Hafkin and Edna Bay (Stanford: Stanford University Press, 1976), p. 224; and Porter, *Creoledom*, p. 86, for a discussion of the importance of class and church affiliation within Krio society.

30. *Daily Mail*, December 16, 1954.

31. Ibid.

32. Theodore Jones, interview with author, September 28, 1976; Abigail Coker-Black, interview with author, March 3, 1976; Judy Vincent, interview with author, October 9, 1976; I. C. Hotobah-During, interview with author, September 27, 1976.

33. Sarah Cole, interview with author, September 22, 1976.

34. T. Jones, interview with author, September 30, 1976.

35. *Daily Mail*, December 16, 1954.

36. Michael Crowder, *West Africa Under Colonial Rule* (London: Hutchinson and Co., 1968), p. 158.

37. Vincent, interview with author, October 9, 1976.

38. T. Jones, interview with author, September 30, 1976.

39. M. C. F. Easmon, "Sierra Leone Doctors," *Sierra Leone Studies* 6 (1955): 49; *Daily Mail*, December 16, 1954; Hotobah-During, interview with author, September 27, 1976; T. Jones, interviews with author, September 28, September 30, December 6, 1976.

40. Peter C. Garlick has noted the importance of the supernatural in the lives of Ghanaian traders and has reported that many Ghanaians believe success or failure in trading is based on the use of witchcraft by or against a trader. *African Traders and Economic Development in Ghana* (London: Clarendon Press, 1971), pp. 107–9. Big Market traders were actually

reluctant to speak about Jones's supernatural powers. Similarly, when discussing another trader who was doing slightly better than others at the time of the research, two vendors moved from speaking Krio to "deep Krio," which contains many Yoruba words. Clearly they did not want the researcher to understand what a research assistant later explained was a discussion of supernatural powers.

41. For a discussion of the role of Christianity in Krio women's lives, see Steady, "Protestant Women's Associations," pp. 213–37.

42. See Johnson, "Marketwomen and Capitalist Adaptation," for a discussion of Benin women who faced similar challenges.

43. S. Cole, interview with author, September 22, 1976; Hotobah-During, interviews with author, September 27, 1976, and August 22, 1983.

Chapter 5

1. Robert A. LeVine, "Sex Roles and Economic Change in Africa," in *Black Africa: Its Peoples and Their Cultures Today*, ed. John Middleton (London: Macmillan and Co., 1970); Niara Sudarkasa, *Where Women Work: A Study of Yoruba Women in the Marketplace and in the Home* (Ann Arbor: University of Michigan, 1973); Phoebe V. Ottenberg, "The Changing Economic Position of Women Among the Afikpo Ibo," in *Continuity and Change in African Cultures*, ed. William R. Bascom and Melville J. Herskovits (Chicago: University of Chicago Press, 1959).

2. LeVine, "Sex Roles and Economic Change," p. 177.

3. S. F. Nadel, "Witchcraft in Four African Societies: A Comparison," *American Anthropologist* 54, no. 4 (1954).

4. LeVine, "Sex Roles and Economic Change," p. 177.

5. Ibid., p. 178.

6. Ottenberg, "The Changing Position of Women."

7. Ibid., p. 314.

8. Sudarkasa, *Where Women Work*, p. 37.

9. An early statement of this view is expressed by the anonymous author of an article entitled "African Women and Their Would-Be Friends," who writes: "It has in some cases been the impact with European civilization that has weakened their [African women's] position. Generally this has been done by cutting the ground, economically, from beneath their feet." *West Africa*, December 4, 1937.

10. Sidney W. Mintz, "Men, Women and Trade," *Comparative Studies in Society and History* 13, no. 3 (1971): 247–69.

11. Paul Bohannon and George Dalton, "Introduction," in *Markets in Africa*, ed. Paul Bohannon and George Dalton (Evanston: Northwestern University Press, 1962), pp. 1–3. Mintz's reliance on Bohannon and

Dalton's argument confuses the issue because of a central weakness in their reasoning. Bohannon and Dalton divide societies into three economic categories: "marketless" societies without marketplaces or market principles; "peripheral" societies where marketplaces exist but the market principle is peripheral, and "market economies" that are dominated by the market principle, defined as "the determination of prices by the forces of supply and demand regardless of the site of transactions" (ibid.). They make it appear that only marketless and peripheral societies are influenced by noneconomic determinants of price. Yet as William G. Davis points out, "to find any market in which 'local institutional peculiarities' did not influence transactions would be difficult. And to the extent that goods are sold on a market, their exchange value is always allocating those factors used in their production. Thus the distinctions drawn between the types are badly blurred." *Social Relations in a Philippine Market: Self-Interest and Subjectivity* (Berkeley: University of California Press, 1973), p. 72.

12. Mintz, "Men, Women and Trade," p. 260.

13. Ibid., pp. 265–66. Mintz maintains that the very nature of salary payments limits women's opportunities for economic independence, but he does not say how or why this is so.

14. Leith Mullings, "Women and Economic Change in Africa," in *Women in Africa: Social and Economic Change*, ed. Nancy Hafkin and Edna Bay (Stanford: Stanford University Press, 1976), pp. 239–64.

15. Ibid., p. 246. For a critique of underdevelopment theory, see Ian Roxborough, *Theories of Underdevelopment* (Atlantic Highlands, N.J.: Humanities Press, 1979). While Roxborough does not address theories of underdevelopment as they apply to women's status, his framework is applicable to this work. Most importantly, writers such as Mullings ignore the stratification of women into classes.

16. Mullings, "Women and Economic Change," p. 248.

17. Ibid., p. 225. Claire Robertson's important work, *Sharing the Same Bowl: A Socioeconomic History of Women and Class in Accra, Ghana* (Bloomington: Indiana University Press, 1984), takes the kind of analysis used by Mullings (and Karen Sacks, *Sisters and Wives: The Past and Future of Sexual Equality* [Urbana: University of Illinois Press, 1982]) a step further. Robertson attacks as myth the formulation that precolonial African cultures were sexually egalitarian. Nonetheless, while she provides a valuable correction to Mullings and a useful chronology of changes in the lives of Ga women from the precolonial to the postcolonial era, she is overly invested in nineteenth-century notions of progress that posit certain stages of development and changes in modes of production as inevitable and near universal. Robertson's work suggests that many of the problems facing scholars in the 1970s continue to plague those who study African

women in the 1980s. See chapter 1 for critiques of feminist analyses that overemphasize a single factor, such as the mode of production, as the major determinant of women's status.

18. Kamene Okonjo, "The Dual-Sex Political System in Operation: Igbo Women and Community Politics in Midwestern Nigeria," and Judith Van Allen, "'Aba Riots' or Igbo 'Women's War'? Ideology, Stratification, and the Invisibility of Women," both in *Women in Africa: Studies in Social and Economic Change,* ed. Nancy Hafkin and Edna Bay (Stanford: Stanford University Press, 1976); Judith Van Allen, "'Sitting on a Man': Colonialism and the Lost Political Institutions of Igbo Women," *Canadian Journal of African Studies* 7, no. 2 (1972): 165–81.

19. Okonjo, "Dual-Sex Political System," p. 45.

20. Ibid., p. 56.

21. Van Allen, "Sitting on a Man," p. 176.

22. N. A. Cox-George, *Finance and Development in West Africa: The Sierra Leone Experience* (London: Denis Dobson, 1961), pp. 27–28. On the Big Market, see chapter 2 above.

23. For a similar argument see the discussion of Benin marketwomen in Eleanor Johnson, "Marketwomen and Capitalist Adaptation: A Case Study of Rural Benin, Nigeria" (Ph.D. diss., Michigan State University, 1974), pp. 163–67.

24. Okonjo, "Dual-Sex Political System," p. 45.

25. Van Allen, "Sitting on a Man," p. 176.

26. James W. St. G. Walker, *The Black Loyalists: The Search for a Promised Land in Nova Scotia and Sierra Leone, 1783–1870* (New York: Africana Publishing Co., 1976), p. 207.

27. *West Africa,* December 6, 1930.

28. *West Africa,* December 27, 1938.

29. Cf. Allen F. Isaacman, *Mozambique: The Africanization of a European Institution, the Zambesi Prazeros, 1750–1902* (Madison: University of Wisconsin Press, 1972).

30. George E. Brooks, Jr., "The *Signares* of Saint-Louis and Gorée: Women Entrepreneurs in Eighteenth-Century Senegal," in *Women in Africa: Studies in Social and Economic Change,* ed. Nancy Hafkin and Edna Bay (Stanford: Stanford University Press, 1976); Philip Curtin, *Economic Change in Precolonial Africa: Senegambia in the Era of the Slave Trade* (Madison: University of Wisconsin Press, 1975); J. M. Gray, *A History of The Gambia* (London: Irwin Press, 1966), chap. 21; Florence Mahoney, "Notes on Mulattoes of The Gambia Before the Mid-Nineteenth Century," *Transactions of the Historical Society of Ghana* 8 (1965).

31. Brooks, "*Signares* of Saint-Louis," p. 19.

32. Ibid., p. 20.

33. Mahoney, "Notes on Mulattoes," p. 125.

34. Brooks, "*Signares* of Saint-Louis," pp. 34–36.

35. Ibid., p. 41.

36. Ibid., p. 44. But as Curtin points out, a fanciful view of signare society should not prevail, for "in spite of the romantic picture sometimes painted of the gay young noblemen and the beautiful signares in the twilight of the old regime, the society was ultimately artificial. It was sustained from the outside by a continuous one-way drain of men from Europe, whose function was to support and further an even larger drain of men from Africa to America," *Economic Change*, p. 120.

37. Abner Cohen, *Custom and Politics in Urban Africa: A Study of Hausa Migrants in Yoruba Towns* (Berkeley: University of California Press, 1969), p. 4. Cohen bases his discussion of the Hausa women almost entirely on interviews with men. This limitation manifests itself in his choice of the word prostitute to describe divorced women who have a good deal of sexual freedom. Such an oversight also raises the questions whether Hausa women would have seen their roles differently and whether men's views of them reflected reality or their own (and Cohen's) ideology.

38. Ibid., p. 51.

39. It may not be that women are any more influential in guarding cultural traditions than men, but that it takes both sexes to create an atmosphere approximating the home culture.

40. Curtin, *Economic Change*, p. 65.

41. Isaacman, *Mozambique;* Allen F. Isaacman and Barbara Isaacman, "The Prazeros as Transfrontiersmen: A Study in Social and Cultural Change," *International Journal of African Historical Studies* 8, no. 1 (1975): 1–39.

42. Isaacman, *Mozambique*, pp. xi–xii.

43. Isaacman and Isaacman, "Prazeros as Transfrontiersmen," p. 2 n.6.

44. Ibid., p. 2.

45. Isaacman, *Mozambique*, p. 60.

46. Ibid., p. 59.

47. Isaacman and Isaacman, "Prazeros as Transfrontiersmen," p. 36.

48. Ibid. Unfortunately, Isaacman and Isaacman give little information about the women whom the prazeros marry, so they do not come to life as do the signares in the Senegambia.

Bibliography

Documents and Reports

Annual Reports for Sierra Leone, 1900–1920. Freetown: Sierra Leone Government.

Church Missionary Society Records, West Africa (CA1), London. Sierra Leone Missionary Reports, Diaries, and Letters, 1830–1901.

Cox-George, N. A. "Report on African Participation in the Commerce of Sierra Leone and the Government Thereon." Freetown: Sierra Leone Government, 1960.

Great Britain. Parliamentary Papers. Vol. 20, 1825–26; vol. 52, 1844; vol. 60, 1899.

————. Public Record Office, London. Sierra Leone: Governors Dispatches to the Secretary of State. Colonial Office 267/1664–1943.

Sierra Leone Government Archives, University of Sierra Leone. Government Interpreters Letter Books, 1885–88.

————. Liberated African Letter Books, 1820–42.

————. Local Letters to the Governor, 1863–79.

————. Native Affairs Letter Books, 1891–98.

————. Native Affairs Minute Papers, 1893–98.

Sierra Leone Legislative Council Debates, 1925–26. Freetown: Sierra Leone Government.

Newspapers

Colonial and Provincial Reporter, 1912–13.

Daily Mail, December 16, 1954.

Sierra Leone Weekly News, 1885–1929.

West Africa, 1919–40.

We Yonne, January 14, 1981.

Books and Articles

Afonja, Simi. "Changing Modes of Production and the Sexual Division of Labour among the Yoruba." *Signs* 7, no. 2 (Winter 1981): 299–313.

Agiri, Babatunde. "The Introduction of Nitida Kola into Nigerian Agriculture, 1880–1920." *African Economic History* 3 (Spring 1977): 1–14.

————. "Slavery in Yoruba Society in the Nineteenth Century." In *The Ideology of Slavery in Africa*, edited by Paul E. Lovejoy. Beverly Hills: Sage Publications, 1980.

Ajayi, J. F. A. "The Aftermath of the Fall of Old Oyo." In *History of West Africa*, edited by J. F. A. Ajayi and Michael Crowder, vol. 2. London: Longman Press, 1974.

Ajayi, J. F. A., and Robert Smith. *Yoruba Warfare in the Nineteenth Century.* Cambridge: Cambridge University Press, 1971.

Akinjobgin, I. A. "The Expansion of Oyo and the Rise of Dahomey, 1600-1800." In *History of West Africa*, edited by J. F. A. Ajayi and Michael Crowder, vol. 1. London: Longman Press, 1971.

Alldridge, Thomas Joshua. *The Sherbro and Its Hinterland.* London: Macmillan and Co., 1901.

Anya, Oji. "The Sherbro in the Nineteenth Century: A Coastal People in Transition." Master's thesis, Fourah Bay College, 1973.

Baier, Stephen B. "African Merchants in the Colonial Period: A History of Commerce in Damagaram (Central Niger), 1880–1960." Ph.D. diss., University of Wisconsin, 1974.

Baier, Stephen, and Paul Lovejoy. "The Desert-Side Economy of the Central Sudan." *International Journal of African Historical Studies* 7, no. 4 (1975): 551–81.

Banbury, G. A. L. *Sierra Leone or the White Man's Grave.* London: S. Sonnenshein, 1888.

Barth, Fredrik. "Introduction." In *Ethnic Groups and Boundaries: The Social Organization of Culture Difference*, edited by Fredrik Barth. Boston: Little, Brown and Co., 1969.

Bastide, Roger. *African Civilizations in the New World.* Translated by Peter Green. New York: Harper and Row, 1971.

Biobaku, Samuel O. *The Egba and Their Neighbors, 1842–1872.* Oxford: Clarendon Press, 1971.

Blassingame, John W. *The Slave Community: Plantation Life in the Antebellum South.* New York: Oxford University Press, 1972.

Bledsoe, Caroline. *Women and Marriage in Kpelle Society.* Stanford: Stanford University Press, 1980.

Bohannon, Paul, and George Dalton. "Introduction." In *Markets in Africa*, edited by Paul Bohannon and George Dalton. Evanston: Northwestern University Press, 1962.

Boserup, Ester. *Woman's Role in Economic Development.* New York: St. Martin's Press, 1970.

Brooks, George E., Jr. "Kola Trade and State-Building: Upper Guinea Coast and Senegambia, 15th to 17th Centuries." African Studies Center Working Papers, no. 38. Boston: Boston University, 1980.

————. "The *Signares* of Saint-Louis and Gorée: Women Entrepreneurs in Eighteenth-Century Senegal." In *Women in Africa: Studies in Social and Economic Change,* edited by Nancy Hafkin and Edna Bay. Stanford: Stanford University Press, 1976.

Bujra, Janet M. "Introductory: Female Solidarity and the Sexual Division of Labour." In *Women United, Women Divided,* edited by Patricia Caplan and Janet M. Bujra. London: Travistock Publications, 1978.

Burton, Richard. *Wanderings in West Africa: From Liverpool to Fernando Po.* 2 vols. London: Tinsley Brothers, 1863.

Butt-Thompson, F. W. *Sierra Leone in History and Tradition.* London: H. F. and G. W. Witherby, 1926.

Campbell, Mavis Christine. "The Maroons of Jamaica: *imperium in imperio?*" *Pan African Journal* 6, no. 1 (Spring 1973): 45–55.

Challenor, Herschelle Sullivan. "Strangers as Colonial Intermediaries: The Dahomeyans in Francophone Africa." In *Strangers in African Societies,* edited by William A. Shack and Elliot P. Skinner. Berkeley: University of California Press, 1979.

Christaller, Walter. *Central Places in Southern Germany.* Translated by Carlisle W. Baskin. Englewood Cliffs, N.J.: Prentice-Hall, 1966.

Church, Mary [pseud.]. *Liberated Africans, In a Series of Letters from a Young Lady to Her Sister in 1833 and 1834.* London: Longman and Co., 1835.

Church, R. J. Harrison. *West Africa: A Study of the Environment and Man's Use of It.* London: Oxford University Press, 1957.

Clapperton, Hugh. *Journal of a Second Expedition into the Interior of Africa from the Bight of Benin to Soccatto.* 1829. Reprint. London: Frank Cass and Co., 1966.

Clarke, J. I., ed. *Sierra Leone in Maps.* London: University of London Press, 1966.

Clarke, Robert. *Sierra Leone: A Description of the Manners and Customs of the Liberated African.* London: James Ridgeway and Co., 1843.

Clarkson, Thomas. "Diary of Thomas Clarkson." *Sierra Leone Studies,* o.s., 8 (1927): 3–10.

Cohen, Abner, "Cultural Strategies in the Organization of Trading Diasporas." In *The Development of Indigenous Trade and Markets in West Africa,* edited by Claude Meillassoux and Daryll Forde. London: Oxford University Press, 1971.

————. *Custom and Politics in Urban Africa: A Study of Hausa Migrants in Yoruba Towns.* Berkeley: University of California Press, 1969.

———. *The Politics of Elite Culture: Explorations in the Dramaturgy of Power in a Modern African Society*. Berkeley: University of California Press, 1981.

———. "The Politics of Ritual Secrecy." *Man* 6 (1971): 427–48.

Cole, Gibril R. "Krio Muslim Society of Freetown: A Case Study of Fourah Bay and Fourah Town, 1810–1910." B.A. honors thesis, Fourah Bay College, 1978.

Cox-George, N. A. *Finance and Development in West Africa: The Sierra Leone Experience*. London: Denis Dobson, 1961.

Crooks, J. J. *A History of the Colony of Sierra Leone*. Dublin: Frank Cass, 1903.

Crowder, Michael. *West Africa Under Colonial Rule*. London: Hutchinson and Co., 1968.

Crowder, Michael, and LaRay Denzer. "Bai Bureh and the Sierra Leone Hut Tax War of 1898." In *Protest and Power in Black Africa*, edited by Robert I. Rotberg and Ali Mazrui. London: Oxford University Press, 1970.

Curtin, Philip D. *Cross-Cultural Trade in World History*. London: Cambridge University Press, 1984.

———. *Economic Change in Precolonial Africa: Senegambia in the Era of the Slave Trade*. Madison: University of Wisconsin Press, 1975.

Dalby, T. D. P. "Language Distribution in Sierra Leone." *Sierra Leone Language Review* 1 (1962): 62–67.

Dallas, Robert Charles. *The History of the Maroons, from Their Origin to the Establishment of Their Chief Tribe at Sierra Leone, etc.* 2 vols. London: Longman and Rees, 1803.

Dalton, K. G. *A Geography of Sierra Leone*. Cambridge: Cambridge University Press, 1965.

Davidson, John. "Trade and Politics in the Sherbro Hinterland, 1849–1890." Ph.D. diss., University of Wisconsin, 1969.

Davies, P. N. *The Trade Makers: Elder Dempster in West Africa, 1852–1972*. London: Allen and Unwin, 1973.

Davis, William G. *Social Relations in a Philippine Market: Self-Interest and Subjectivity*. Berkeley: University of California Press, 1973.

Denzer, LaRay, and Leo Spitzer. "I. T. A. Wallace-Johnson and the West African Youth League." *International Journal of African Historical Studies* 6, nos. 3–4 (1973): 413–52; 565–601.

Deveneux, Gustav K. "The Political and Social Impact of the Colony in Northern Sierra Leone, 1821–1896." Ph.D. diss., Boston University, 1973.

Dewey, Alice G. *Peasant Marketing in Java*. Glencoe, Ill.: Free Press, 1962.

Dorjahn, V. R. and Christopher Fyfe. "Landlord and Stranger: Change in Tenancy Relations in Sierra Leone." *Journal of African History* 3, no. 3 (1962): 391–97.

Easmon, M. C. F. "Sierra Leone Doctors." *Sierra Leone Studies*, n.s., 6 (1965): 81–96.

Ekejuiba, Felicia, "Omu Okwesi, the Merchant Queen of Ossomari: A Biographical Sketch." *Journal of the Historical Society of Nigeria* 3, no. 4 (1967): 633–46.

Engels, Frederick. *The Origin of the Family, Private Property and the State.* New York: International Publishers, 1972.

Fitch-Jones, B. W. "Extracts from a Diary Written During the 1898 Rebellion." *Sierra Leone Studies*, o.s., 17 (1932): 13–17.

Flickinger, Daniel K. *Ethiopia Coming to God: Missionary Life in West Africa.* Dayton: United Brethren Printing Establishment, 1877.

———. *The History of the Origin, Development and Condition of Missions among the Sherbro and Mendi Tribes in Western Africa.* Dayton: United Brethren Printing Establishment, 1880.

———. *Off Hand Sketches of Men and Things in Western Africa.* Dayton: United Brethren Printing Establishment, 1957.

Forde, Daryll, *The Yoruba-Speaking Peoples of South-Western Nigeria.* London: International African Institute, 1962.

Fyfe, Christopher. "European and Creole Influences in the Hinterland of Sierra Leone before 1896." *Sierra Leone Studies*, n.s., no. 6 (1956): 113–23.

———. *A History of Sierra Leone.* London: Oxford University Press, 1962.

———. "Reform in West Africa: The Abolition of the Slave Trade." In *History of West Africa*, edited by J. F. A. Ajayi and Michael Crowder, vol. 2. New York: Columbia University Press, 1972.

Fyle, C. Magbaily. *The History of Sierra Leone: A Concise Introduction.* London: Evans Brothers, 1981.

———. "Precolonial Commerce in Northeastern Sierra Leone." African Studies Center Working Papers, no. 10. Boston: Boston University, 1979.

———. *The Solima Yalunka Kingdom: Pre-Colonial Politics, Economics and Society.* Freetown: Nyakon Publishers, 1979.

Gardner, William James. *A History of Jamaica from Its Discovery by Christopher Columbus to the Year 1872.* London: n.p., n.d.

Garlick, Peter C. *African Traders and Economic Development in Ghana.* London: Clarendon Press, 1971.

Genovese, Eugene D. *Roll, Jordan, Roll: The World the Slaves Made.* New York: Pantheon Books, 1974.

Gray, J. M. *A History of The Gambia.* London: Irwin Press, 1966.

Gulliver, Adelaide Cromwell. "A Biographical Approach to the Study of African Women in Twentieth Century Socio-Economic Change." Paper presented at the UCLA African Studies Center Colloquium on Women and Change in Africa, 1870–1970, Los Angeles, April, 1974.

Gutman, Herbert G. *The Black Family in Slavery and Freedom, 1750–1925*. New York: Vintage Books, 1977.

Hanna, Marwan. "The Lebanese in West Africa." *West Africa*, no. 2142 (May 3, 1958): 369, 393, 415, 417, 463, 487.

Hargraves, John D. *A Life of Sir Samuel Lewis*. London: Oxford University Press, 1958.

Harrell-Bond, Barbara, Allen Howard, and David Skinner. *Community Leadership and the Transformation of Freetown (1801–1976)*. The Hague: Mouton Publishers, 1978.

Harvey, Milton. "Bonthe: A Geographical Study of a Moribund Port and Its Environs." *Bulletin of the Journal of the Sierra Leone Association* 10 (1966): 60–75.

Headrick, Daniel R. *The Tools of Empire: Technology and European Imperialism in the Nineteenth Century*. New York: Oxford University Press, 1981.

Hinckley, Priscilla. "The Sowo Mask: Symbol of Sisterhood." African Studies Center Working Papers, no. 40. Boston: Boston University, 1980.

Hobsbawm, E. J. "From Social History to the History of Society." *Daedalus* 100, no. 1 (1971): 20–45.

Hodder, B. W., and U. J. Ukwu. *Markets in West Africa*. Ibadan, Nigeria: Ibadan University Press, 1969.

Hoffer, Carol P. "Bundu: Political Implications of Female Solidarity in a Secret Society." In *Being Female: Reproduction, Power, and Change*, edited by Dana Raphael. The Hague: Mouton Publishers, 1975.

———. "Mende and Sherbro Women in High Office." *Canadian Journal of African Studies* 6, no. 2 (1972): 287–303.

Holsoe, Svend E. "Slavery and Economic Response Among the Vai (Liberia and Sierra Leone)." In *Slavery in Africa: Historical and Anthropological Perspectives*, edited by Suzanne Miers and Igor Kopytoff. Madison: University of Wisconsin Press, 1977.

Hopkins, Anthony G. *An Economic History of West Africa*. New York: Columbia University Press, 1973.

Horton, James Africanus Beale. *West African Countries and Peoples*. 1868. Reprint. Edinburgh: Edinburgh University Press, 1969.

Howard, Allen M. "Big Men, Traders, and Chiefs: Power, Commerce and Spatial Change in the Sierra Leone–Guinea Plain, 1865–1895." Ph.D. diss., University of Wisconsin, 1972.

———. "Historical Centralities and Spatial Patterns in Northern Sierra Leone." Paper presented at the Joint Committee on African Studies of the American Council of Learned Societies/Social Science Research Council Conference on Spatial Hierarchies in African Interurban Systems, New York, 1970.

———. "Kola Production and Trade in Sierra Leone, 1850–1930." Paper presented at the University Of London School of Oriental and African Studies and Institute of Commonwealth Studies, May 16, 1979.

———. "The Relevance of Spatial Analysis for African Economic History: The Sierra Leone–Guinea System." *Journal of African History* 17 (1976): 365–88.

———. "The Role of Freetown in the Commercial Life of Sierra Leone." In *Freetown: A Symposium*, edited by Christopher Fyfe and Eldred Jones. Freetown: University of Sierra Leone Press, 1966.

Howard, Rhoda. *Colonialism and Underdevelopment in Ghana*. New York: Africana Publishing Co., 1978.

Ingham, E. G. *Sierra Leone After a Hundred Years*. London: Seely and Co., 1894.

Isaacman, Allen F. *Mozambique: The Africanization of a European Institution, the Zambesi Prazeros, 1750–1902*. Madison: University of Wisconsin Press, 1972.

Isaacman, Allen F., and Barbara Isaacman. "The Prazeros as Transfrontiersmen: A Study in Social and Cultural Change." *International Journal of African Historical Studies*, 8, no. 1 (1975): 1–39.

Johnson, Eleanor. "Marketwomen and Capitalist Adaptation: A Case Study of Rural Benin, Nigeria." Ph.D. diss., Michigan State University, 1974.

Johnson, Samuel. *The History of the Yorubas from the Earliest Times to the Beginning of the British Protectorate*. London: Church Missionary Society, 1921.

Jones, Adam. *From Slaves to Palm Kernels: A History of the Galinhas Country (West Africa), 1730–1890*. Wiesbaden: Steiner, 1983.

Kaniki, Martin H. Y. "Attitudes and Reactions towards the Lebanese in Sierra Leone during the Colonial Period." *Canadian Journal of African Studies* 8, no. 1 (1973): 97–113.

Kilson, Martin. *Political Change in a West African State: A Study of the Modernization Process in Sierra Leone*. Cambridge: Harvard University Press, 1966.

Klein, Martin K. "The Decolonization of West African History." *Journal of Interdisciplinary History* 6, no. 1 (1975): 111–25.

Knight, Franklin W. *The African Dimension in Latin American Societies*. New York: Macmillan Co., 1974.

Kopytoff, Barbara K. "The Maroons of Jamaica: An Ethnohistorical Study of Incomplete Politics." Ph.D. diss., University of Pennsylvania, 1973.

Kreutzinger, Helga. "The Markets of Freetown." Sierra Leone Government Archives, 1966.

Law, Robin. *The Oyo Empire, c. 1600–c. 1836: A West African Imperialism in the Era of the Atlantic Slave Trade*. Oxford: Clarendon Press, 1977.

Leighton, Neil Owen. "Lebanese Middlemen in Sierra Leone: The Case of a Non-Indigenous Trading Minority and Their Role in Political Development." Ph.D. diss., Indiana University, 1971.

————. "The Political Economy of a Stranger Population: The Lebanese of Sierra Leone." In *Strangers in African Societies,* edited by William A. Shack and Elliot P. Skinner. Berkeley: University of California Press, 1979.

Lemise, Jesse. "The American Revolution Seen from the Bottom Up." In *Toward a New Past: Dissenting Essays in American History,* edited by Barton J. Bernstein. New York: Pantheon Books, 1968.

Levine, Donald N. "Simmel at a Distance: On the History and Systematics of the Sociology of the Stranger." In *Strangers in African Societies,* edited by William A. Shack and Elliot P. Skinner. Berkeley: University of California Press, 1979.

LeVine, Robert A. "Sex Roles and Economic Change in Africa." In *Black Africa: Its Peoples and Cultures Today,* edited by John Middleton. London: Macmillan and Co., 1970.

Little, Kenneth L. "The Changing Position of Women in the Sierra Leone Protectorate." *Africa* 18, no. 4 (1948): 1–17.

Losch, A. *The Economics of Location.* Translated by W. H. Woylon. New Haven: Yale University Press, 1954.

Lovejoy, Paul E. "The Hausa Kola Trade (1700–1900): A Commercial System in the Continental Exchange of West Africa." Ph.D. diss., University of Wisconsin, 1973.

————. "Slavery in the Context of Ideology." In *The Ideology of Slavery in Africa,* edited by Paul E. Lovejoy. Beverly Hills: Sage Publications, 1980.

————. *Transformations in Slavery: A History of Slavery in Africa.* Cambridge: Cambridge University Press, 1983.

McCall, Daniel F. "The Koforidua Market." In *Markets in Africa,* edited by Paul Bohannon and George Dalton. Evanston: Northwestern University Press, 1962.

MacCormack, Carol P. "Wono: Institutionalized Dependency in Sherbro Descent Groups." In *Slavery in Africa: Historical and Anthropological Perspectives,* edited by Suzanne Miers and Igor Kopytoff. Madison: University of Wisconsin Press, 1977.

Mahoney, Florence K. Omolara. "Government and Opinion in The Gambia, 1816–1901." Ph.D. diss., London University, 1963.

————. "Notes on Mulattoes of The Gambia Before the Mid-Nineteenth Century." *Transactions of the Historical Society of Ghana* 8 (1965): 120–29.

Melville, Elizabeth. *A Residence at Sierra Leone.* London: John Murray, 1849.

Milton, Harvey. "Bonthe: A Geographical Study of a Moribund Port and Its Environs." *Bulletin of the Journal of the Sierra Leone Association,* no. 10 (1966): 60–75.

Mintz, Sidney W. "Men, Women and Trade." *Comparative Studies in Society and History* 13, no. 3 (1971): 247–69.

Mintz, Sidney, and Richard Price. *An Anthropological Approach to the Afro-American Past: A Caribbean Perspective.* Philadelphia: Institute for the Study of Human Issues, 1977.

Mitchell, P. K. "Freetown as a Port." In *Freetown: A Symposium,* edited by Christopher Fyfe and Eldred Jones. Freetown: University of Sierra Leone Press, 1968.

Mullings, Leith. "Women and Economic Change in Africa." In *Women in Africa: Social and Economic Change,* edited by Nancy Hafkin and Edna Bay. Stanford: Stanford University Press, 1976.

Nadel, S. F. "Witchcraft in Four African Societies: A Comparison." *American Anthropologist* 54, no. 4 (1954): 18–29.

Newland, H. Osman. *Sierra Leone: Its People, Products, and Secret Societies.* London: John Bale and Sons and Danielson, 1916.

Nkrumah, Kwame. *Ghana: An Autobiography.* Edinburgh: Thomas Nelson, 1959.

Okonjo, Kamene. "The Dual-Sex Political System in Operation: Igbo Women and Community Politics in Midwestern Nigeria." In *Women in Africa: Studies in Social and Economic Change,* edited by Nancy Hafkin and Edna Bay. Stanford: Stanford University Press, 1976.

———. "Women's Political Participation in Nigeria." In *The Black Woman Cross-Culturally,* edited by Filomina Chioma Steady. Cambridge, Mass.: Schenkman Publishing Co., 1981.

Olu-Wright, R. J. "The Physical Growth of Freetown." In *Freetown: A Symposium,* edited by Christopher Fyfe and Eldred Jones. Freetown: University of Sierra Leone Press, 1968.

Ortner, Sherry B. "Is Female to Male as Nature is to Culture?" In *Woman, Culture, and Society,* edited by Michelle Z. Rosaldo and Louise Lamphere. Stanford: Stanford University Press, 1974.

Ortner, Sherry B., and Harriet Whitehead. "Introduction: Accounting for Sexual Meanings." In *Sexual Meanings: The Cultural Construction of Gender and Sexuality,* edited by Sherry B. Ortner and Harriet Whitehead. Cambridge: Cambridge University Press, 1981.

Ottenberg, Phoebe V. "The Changing Economic Position of Women Among the Afikpo Ibo." In *Continuity and Change in African Cultures,* edited by William R. Bascom and Melville J. Herskovits. Chicago: University of Chicago Press, 1959.

Patterson, Orlando. "Slavery and Slave Revolts: A Sociohistorical Analysis of the First Maroon War, Jamaica, 1655–1740." *Social and Economic Studies* 19, no. 3 (September, 1970): 289–325.

Peterson, John. "Independence and Innovation in the Nineteenth Century Colony Village." *Sierra Leone Studies,* n.s., 21 (July 1967): 2–11.

———. *Province of Freedom: A History of Sierra Leone, 1787–1870.* London: Faber and Faber, 1969.

———. "The Sierra Leone Creole: A Reappraisal." In *Freetown: A Symposium,* edited by Christopher Fyfe and Eldred Jones. Freetown: University of Sierra Leone Press, 1968.

Phillip, Robert. *The Life, Times and Missionary Enterprises of Rev. Campbell.* London: John Snow, 1841.

Porter, Arthur T. *Creoledom: A Study of the Development of Freetown Society.* Oxford: Oxford University Press, 1963.

Rankin, F. Harrison. *The White Man's Grave: A Visit to Sierra Leone in 1834.* 2 vols. London: Richard Bentley, 1836.

Rawick, George P. *From Sundown to Sunup: The Making of the Black Community.* Westport, Conn.: Greenwood Press, 1972.

Reade, Winwood. *The African Sketch-Book.* 2 vols. London: Smith, Elder and Co., 1873.

Robertson, Claire. "Economic Woman in Africa: Profit-Making Techniques of Accra Market Women." *Journal of Modern African Studies* 12, no. 4 (December 1974): 657–64.

———. *Sharing the Same Bowl: A Socioeconomic History of Women and Class in Accra, Ghana.* Bloomington: Indiana University Press, 1984.

Robertson, Claire, and Martin A. Klein. "Women's Importance in African Slave Systems." In *Women and Slavery in Africa,* edited by Claire Robertson and Martin A. Klein. Madison: University of Wisconsin Press, 1983.

Rodney, Walter. *A History of the Upper Guinea Coast, 1545 to 1800.* London: Oxford University Press, 1970.

Rosaldo, Michelle Z. "The Use and Abuse of Anthropology: Reflections on Feminism and Cross-Cultural Understanding." *Signs* 5, no. 3 (1980): 389–417.

———. "Woman, Culture and Society: A Theoretical Overview." In *Woman, Culture, and Society,* edited by Michelle Rosaldo and Louise Lamphere. Stanford: Stanford University Press, 1974.

Roxborough, Ian. *Theories of Underdevelopment.* Atlantic Highlands, N.J.: Humanities Press, 1979.

Sacks, Karen. *Sisters and Wives: The Past and Future of Sexual Equality.* Urbana: University of Illinois Press, 1982.

Shack, William A. "Introduction." In *Strangers in African Societies,* edited by

William A. Shack and Elliot P. Skinner. Berkeley: University of California Press, 1979.

Sibthorpe, A. B. C. *The History of Sierra Leone.* London: Elliot Stock, 1881.

Simmel, Georg. "The Stranger." In *The Sociology of George Simmel,* translated and edited by Kurt H. Wolf. New York: Free Press, 1950.

Skinner, David E. *Thomas George Lawson: African Historian and Administrator in Sierra Leone.* Stanford: Hoover Institution Press, 1980.

Skinner, David E., and Barbara E. Harrell-Bond. "Misunderstandings Arising From the Use of the Term 'Creole' in the Literature on Sierra Leone." *Africa* 47, no. 3 (1977): 305–20.

Skinner, Elliot P. "Conclusions." In *Strangers in African Societies,* edited by William A. Shack and Elliot P. Skinner. Berkeley: University of California Press, 1979.

Smart, Joko H. M. "Inheritance to Property in Sierra Leone: An Analysis of the Law and Problems Involved." *Sierra Leone Studies,* n.s., no. 24 (January, 1969): 2–25.

Spitzer, Leo. *The Creoles of Sierra Leone: Responses to Colonialism, 1870–1949.* Madison: University of Wisconsin Press, 1974.

Steady, Filomina Chioma. "Protestant Women's Associations in Freetown, Sierra Leone." In *Women in Africa: Studies in Social and Economic Change,* edited by Nancy Hafkin and Edna Bay. Stanford: Stanford University Press, 1976.

Sudarkasa, Niara. "Female Employment and Family Organization in West Africa." In *The Black Woman Cross-Culturally,* edited by Filomina Chioma Steady. Cambridge, Mass.: Schenkman Publishing Co., 1981.

––––––. *Where Women Work: A Study of Yoruba Women in the Marketplace and in the Home.* Ann Arbor: University of Michigan, 1973.

Trager, Lillian. "Customers and Credit: Variations in Economic Personalism in a Nigerian Market System." *Ethnology* 20, no. 2 (April, 1981): 133–46.

Van Allen, Judith. "'Aba Riots' or Igbo 'Women's War'? Ideology, Stratification, and the Invisibility of Women." In *Women in Africa: Studies in Social and Economic Change,* edited by Nancy Hafkin and Edna Bay. Stanford: Stanford University Press, 1976.

––––––. "'Sitting on a Man': Colonialism and the Lost Political Institutions of Igbo Women." *Canadian Journal of African Studies* 6, no. 2 (1972): 165–81.

van der Laan, H. L. *The Lebanese Traders in Sierra Leone.* The Hague: Mouton Publishers, 1976.

Walker, James W. St. G. *The Black Loyalists: The Search for a Promised Land in Nova Scotia and Sierra Leone, 1783–1870.* New York: Africana Publishing Co., 1976.

Webster, J. B. "Political Activity in British West Africa, 1900–1940." In *History of West Africa*, vol. 2, edited by J. F. A. Ajayi and Michael Crowder. London: Longman Press, 1974.

Whyte, Martin King. *The Status of Women in Preindustrial Societies*. Princeton: Princeton University Press, 1978.

Wilson, Ellen Gibson. *The Loyal Blacks*. New York: G. P. Putnam's Sons, 1976.

Winder, R. Bayly. "The Lebanese in West Africa." *Comparative Studies in Sociology and History* 4 (1962): 296–333.

Winks, Robin W. *The Blacks in Canada: A History*. New Haven: Yale University Press, 1971.

Wood, Peter. *Black Majority: Negroes in Colonial South Carolina from 1670 through the Stono Rebellion*. New York: W. W. Norton and Co., 1975.

———. "'It was a Negro Taught Them.' A Look at African Labor in Early South Carolina." *Journal of Asian and African Studies* 9, nos. 3 and 4 (1974): 160–79.

Wyse, Akintola J. G. "Sierra Leone Creoles: Their History and Historians." *Journal of African Studies* 4, no. 2 (Summer 1977): 228–39.

List of Interviewees

Name	*Town*
Aruna-Tucker, John	Bonthe
Bamiba, John	Bonthe
Beckley, Elizabeth	Kent
Beckles, Mary	Freetown
Benjamins, O. Willis	Freetown
Bull, Onika Clarrisa	Freetown
Clarke, Mirian	Bonthe
Cline, Laura Hero	Freetown
Coker, Farian	Freetown
Coker, Miranda	Freetown
Coker-Black, Abigail	Freetown
Cole, Jonnetta	Kent
Cole, Mirian	Freetown
Cole, Sarah	Freetown
Cowan, Magdeline	Leicester
Cummings-John, Constance	Freetown
Davies, Margaret	Freetown
Davis, Sally	Bonthe
Decker, Anna	Leicester

Decker, Edna	Leicester
Deen, Hannah	Waterloo
Domingo, Lillie Mae	Bonthe
During, Sarian	Leicester
Fraser, Gertrude Ayikulaula	Freetown
George, P. A.	Freetown
Goodman, Reginal	Waterloo
Hollis, Ruth	Leicester
Hotobah-During, I. C.	Freetown
James, Princess	Freetown
James, Tunde	Freetown
Jarrett, Elizabeth	Bonthe
Johnson, Charlotte	Freetown
Johnson, Marie	Tumbo
Johnson, Vivi	Freetown
Johnston-Taylor, Joko	Freetown
Jones, Lucinda O.	Waterloo
Jones, Theodore	Freetown
Jesu, Deborah	Bonthe
Luke, Stella	Bonthe
Macarthy, J. S.	Tumbo
Macauley, Betsy	Leicester
Mansaray, Mary	Bonthe
Morgan, Elizabeth	Bonthe
Morgan, William	Bonthe
Nyula, Mariama	Freetown
Palmer, Bure	Freetown
Palmer, Jennette	Freetown
Pratt, Dinah	Freetown
Robinson, P. Allizas	Freetown
Robinson, William	Freetown
Scott, Sarah	Sussex
Short, Beatrice Victoria	Freetown
Slowe, Josephine	York
Smith, George	Leicester
Spain, Deborah	Bonthe
Thomas, Gwen	Sussex
Thomas, Jane	Freetown
Tucker, Lucy	Bonthe
Vincent, Judy	Freetown
Weeks, M. A.	Regent

Williams, G. J. Akundia	Sussex
Williams, Lucy	Sussex
Williams, Mary	Leicester
Williams, Peter	Bonthe
Wright, Ruth C.	Freetown

Index

Abarimoko, 95
Aboise, Mami. *See* Vincent, Judy Victoria
Afikpo Igbo, 104
Afonja, Simi, 28
African beliefs
  colony women and, 50
  settler cultures and, 8, 20, 24
  support of wives and, 32
African culture. *See also* Colony women: as cultural intermediaries
  Afro-American culture and, 8–9
  European observers and, 123n. 48
  influences from indigenous, 10–11
  precolonial, 140n. 17
  Sierra Leonean historiography and, 6–7
African elite, postwar economic decline and, 61–62
Afro-American culture
  African survivals in, 8–9
  Krio culture and, 8
  marriage bonds and, 119n. 25
  sex roles and, 19–20
Afro-European trade, 30, 121n. 4
Afro-Jamaicans. *See* Aku
Ajayi, Borbor, 96–97
Aku. *See also* Krios
  culture of, 27

  female economic autonomy and, 23
  Islam and, 27
  in Kissy village, 34
  Krio identity and, 3
  origin of term, 124n. 50
  women as traders, 27
Alafin, 29
Alldridge, Joshua T., 45, 46
All-Peoples' Congress (APC), 91
American Mende Mission, 46
Anti-Lebanese riots. *See* Anti-Syrian riots
Anti-Syrian riots, 70–71, 75
APC. *See* All-Peoples' Congress
APC Women's Movement, 91
Apprenticeship system
  Accra market women and, 137n. 4
  as education, 98
  European marriage forms and, 33–34
  function of, 123n. 44
  illiteracy and, 137n. 4
Autonomy. *See* Economic independence; Independence; Sexual autonomy
Ayabas, 29

Barter trade, displacement of, 59
Barth, Fredrik, 7
Bathurst, 69, 87–89, 90
Beah Boy, 57